Always Give a Penny to a Blind Man

Always Give a Penny to a Blind Man

A MEMOIR

Eric Wright

KEY PORTER BOOKS

Canadian Cataloguing in Publication Data

Wright, Eric
    Always give a penny to a blind man

ISBN 1-55263-067-6

1. Wright, Eric.   2. Working Class – England – Biography.   3. Novelists, Canadian (English) – 20th century – Biography.*   I. Title.

PS8595.R58Z53 1999   C813'.54   C99-931097-6
PR9199.3.W66Z463 1999

THE CANADA COUNCIL | LE CONSEIL DES ARTS
FOR THE ARTS | DU CANADA
SINCE 1957 | DEPUIS 1957

The publisher gratefully acknowledges the support of the Canada Council for the Arts and the Ontario Arts Council for its publishing program.

Canadä

We acknowledge the financial support of the Government of Canada through the Book Publishing Industry Development Program (BPIDP) for our publishing activities.

Key Porter Books Limited
70 The Esplanade
Toronto, Ontario
Canada M5E 1R2

www.keyporter.com

Electronic formatting: Heidi Palfrey
Design: Peter Maher

Printed and bound in Canada

99 00 01 02 03 6 5 4 3 2 1

Some of the following,
often in very different form, has appeared in
*The New Yorker, Punch, Descant, Books in Canada,
The Idler, Waterloo Review*

My Thanks

To Ray Hampton and Bert Churcher, schoolmates, who helped me to remember the days at Mitcham County School for Boys.

To my family in England, who scratched together a tiny family archive for me, and told me some of the stories again.

To my wife, Valerie, who has heard these stories so often, for listening one more time.

To Bella Pomer, my agent, for indulging me through the years that this book was finding its shape.

To Anna Porter, my publisher, who told me what that shape was.

To Patrick Crean, my editor, who guided the book past the last rocks with extraordinary skill and tact.

And finally, to my niece, Susan, who asked me, when my brother Len (her father) died, to write something about his family, and is therefore as responsible as anyone for this book.

Table of Contents

For Tory and Jessica

One

The Buildings

SOME THINGS are not in dispute.

I was born in Flat 58, The Buildings, Kennington Park Road, London, S.E. The proper name of the Buildings is Guinness's Buildings, put up, Dad said, out of the profits made from selling stout to him and his mates. He had a lot of sayings like that. "It's the mustard I leave on my plate that makes Colman rich," he said, every time he helped himself.

"Be a long time waiting to get rich out of the mustard *you* leave," Mum said.

"Every little helps."

"So you've told us a thousand times," Mum said in that voice she used when she thought he was talking silly. "Now eat your kipper and let me clean up the kitchen."

Mum also helped Guinness get rich. She drank half a pint every day when her morning's work was done, prescribed by the doctor for her health.

She was a tailoress and Dad was a carter, with a big van and four horses. Before my sister Vi got married there were twelve of us, Mum, Dad, and ten children, a new one born every two years, regular as clockwork, all living together in one flat. There were four blocks of flats at our end of the Buildings, two on each side of the square. Mum called one of the other blocks the "funny block" because some of the people who lived there suffered from fits, or limped a bit. Or worse. "I don't want you to go near the funny block, you hear?" Mum used to say. "I'm warning you. If I catch you near there, I'll give you a clump round the ear."

On Saturday nights the superintendent lit the big boiler at the back of the square, and the men lined up at the tap to get hot water, as many buckets as you wanted. Sometimes I went with Dad down into the square to watch the men line up. Dad carried the water up the stairs, two buckets at a time, making me go in front so he didn't splash boiling water on me. He poured the water into the bath, which clanged when we stepped into it. Then he washed us, me and Jean first, with yellow Sunlight soap. He put washing soda in the water to get us properly clean, but it never melted completely so it was like sitting on the pebbles at the seaside. The water was too hot at first, so that it would still be warm enough for Len and Ron's turn, and when we got out of the bath we were red and shiny and hard from the middle down, and the marks of the unmelted washing soda showed on my bum. In the winter, Mum dried us off in front of the fire with a towel she'd kept warming on the fire screen.

We played in the square while it was light; when it got dark the superintendent came out of his little office in the middle of the square and blew his whistle to send us home. There was a railing all round the Buildings, with a gate that the superintendent locked at bedtime. When Vi's young man brought her home in the evening, the superintendent waited by the gate for him to go home.

I was not allowed through the gate out on to the road, but on Saturday afternoons Dad sent me to buy an afternoon paper with the latest racing results from the man who had a newspaper pitch outside the railings. I held a penny through the railings and he pushed the paper through after he had my penny. New papers came out after each race and some Saturdays Dad bought six.

Gladys took me to infants' school in Crampton Road. In the afternoon at school we had to try to sleep under red blankets. When we closed our eyes, the teacher picked her nose with the corner of her handkerchief. I thought that must be proper manners, something my sisters talked about a lot.

While I was still in infants' school, my brother Joe took me and my little sister Jean a long way away on the Underground to our new house in Colliers Wood, practically in the country. My mum stayed in the Buildings to make sure that all the furniture was moved properly. Ron and Len rode in the van with the movers, and all the others came home to the new house after work.

There was a field behind the house, and a big allotment on one side full of Brussels sprouts and cabbages, so it really seemed like the country. There was a piece of wood hanging from two little chains over the front door with the name of the house, Boomewood, burnt into it with a red-hot poker, but most of the letters we got just said 60 Colwood Gardens. The house was the last one on the street so we had a side path, a front garden, and a back garden. The taps in the bathroom were marked Hot and Cold, but there wasn't any hot water, so on Friday nights Mum lit the gas under the copper in the kitchen and Dad carried the buckets of hot water upstairs for our baths. Dad still put in washing soda, but the bathtub was whiter and smoother than the one in the Buildings so it was easy to clear a space to sit in, free from the soda, and it didn't clang when you stepped into it. My older sisters, who went to work, heated up their own bathwater, and gave Mum twopence or threepence for the extra amount of gas they used. On Saturdays my sisters used to argue over who got the bath first.

Vi got married while we were in the Buildings, but all the rest of us fitted into the new house in Colliers Wood. The four big sisters slept in the back room upstairs, two in a double bed and Doris and Gladys head to toe in a single bed. Mum and Dad had the other bedroom and Joe got the little room they called "the box room." There was no fire-place in the box room, so when Joe got the flu, Mum put two hot-water bottles in his bed. Ron and Len slept on a pull-out couch in the dining room which was also the living room, where there was a fire going until we all went to bed. Jean and I slept on each end of a camp cot on the upstairs landing, but if we were ill, Mum lit a fire in her and Dad's bedroom and Dad moved our cot in there. The front room downstairs was kept for best, for Sundays and Christmas. It was smash-ing having our own house with a front room kept for best.

The rent of the new house was thirty shillings a week. On Saturday mornings the rent collector came to the door in an over-coat down to his ankles that was all holes and had the lining show-ing at the bottom. He wore glasses with only one earpiece and signed the rent-book with a bit of pencil. Mum said he got himself up like this to look poverty-stricken, but everyone knew who he was, and one Saturday a gang of kids jumped on him in the alley by the recre-ation ground and bashed him over the head with an iron poker and took his money. Everyone said it was that gang on Fortescue Road, and the police came round to our house because our Ron sometimes went with the Fortescue Road gang, but this time Ron was miles away with another mate, probably Joey Richards. When he came home Mum warned him anyway what she would do to him if she ever caught him with that gang.

Colwood Gardens was newer than Clarendon Road or Fortescue Road, and the builder tried to keep out families with too many kids so as not to lower the tone. The families on our street all signed a form saying that they had no more than six kids. When the rent collector came, Mum told us to stay clear of the house so he couldn't count how many of us there were. If there seemed to be a lot of us about, Mum pretended to be cross and shouted out to a couple of my brothers, "Clear off, go home to your own house."

Fortescue Road, where the gang who bashed the rent collector lived, was a much older and rougher street. Some of the people there made a living with a horse and cart, hauling rubbish and doing small moving jobs. One of them sold cats' meat from the kind of pony-cart you stand up in—"Pussy's Butcher," he called himself—and another one came round on a tricycle cart selling American coloured comics, which you couldn't buy in the shops, and two-a-penny razor blades. The comics came over as ship's ballast, Dad said. They weren't like our comics, *Dandy* and *Beano*. These had American people in them, *Dick Tracy* and *Blondie* and *The Katzenjammer Kids*. None of them made much sense, though I liked the drawings in *Smokey Stover*.

On Saturday nights some of the people who lived on Fortescue Road came back from the pub and knocked each other about. It was worse than the Buildings, where at least they didn't allow fighting, Mum said.

Dad didn't like Colliers Wood. He was born in Westminster, "over the water," and lived all his life there, or in Vauxhall or in Lambeth, right next door. Where we came from, everyone was the same, ordinary working people, he said, but Colwood Gardens was full of clerks in bowler hats who went up to London on "business," toffy-nosed buggers who thought they were too good for someone who only wore a tie on Saturday nights or when one of his daughters got married.

But his own dad wasn't a Londoner. Grandad had walked down from the north of England in Queen Victoria's day, in the year of the Golden Jubilee in 1887, he claimed, looking for work. He got a job as a pot-boy in a Blackfriars pub, collecting up the dirty glasses and mugs and wiping off the tables. There he met my grandmother who sold flowers outside Blackfriars station during the week, and took her flower basket round the Vauxhall pubs on Saturdays and Sundays. Before long he was helping her, keeping the other flower-sellers away from her pitch, and travelling with her first thing in the morning to Covent Garden for the flowers she sold.

They bought a licence and got married in the registry office and set up house in two rooms in Westminster, where they had three children. She carried on selling flowers, leaving the babies to be looked after by a neighbour, and they saved up the money to buy Grandad a hand barrow, the kind with two wheels and two legs, so that he could do moving jobs. He was very strong—Mum said he could walk downstairs with a piano on his back.

Sometimes on Sunday mornings Dad took me with him on a tram from Colliers Wood to visit his mum and dad over the water in Westminster. Actually Dad's real mum was dead now and this was his stepmother. She was the only stepmother I knew except the wicked kind in stories. When I asked him, Dad said she could be a bit wicked sometimes but not often. They still lived in two rooms in a building older than the Buildings, one which smelled of old people and Brussels sprouts. When we came, Grandma gave me a biscuit and a glass of "Tizer," which I liked better than lemonade; Grandad gave me a threepenny bit. She was Catholic and Grandad said she was always trying to get him to convert. Mum said it was the only thing on Grandad's mind. He told Dad Grandma had a priest waiting who would try to convert him on his deathbed. I wondered if the priest waited in the little cupboard under the stairs where the gas meter was.

Dad had no other family. His brother died of fish-poisoning before he was properly grown up, and his sister, a lady's maid, went down on the *Lusitania*. Mum said that Grandma Wright was a hard woman to have put her only daughter into service, which meant working until you dropped in a scullery full of black beetles. She said Dad's sister was lucky to have been a lady's maid but it was still slavery. When she was fed up with kids saying "can I have this, can I have that" all day long,

Mum said if we didn't give her a bit of peace, she would put my sisters into service to get them off her hands, but she never meant it.

Sometimes, after we had been to visit Gran and Grandad, Dad took me to his stables at Kennington Cross to see the horses he drove all week. Dad's horses were in the upstairs part of the stables, up a long wooden slope. They were much bigger than the horses that the milkman or the baker had to pull their carts, and it was smashing to stroke them in the dark, saying their names, knowing they were Dad's. They had his smell, except for the Woodbines he used to smoke.

Dad was different here to the way he was at home. His mates took more notice of him than we did. He even had a different name. Mum called him Jack, which, she said, was the proper nickname for anyone called Joseph. But at work he was known as Bosher. "'Allo, Bosher," the watchman on the stable gate would say as we went in to the stable yard. And at work Dad could shout across the street if he liked. "'Allo, Tubby," he would call, if he saw someone he knew. "You all right, then?"

Mum didn't like him shouting like that in public. It was common, she said. "Common" meant having no class, like not knowing your manners. It didn't matter much in the Buildings, because everyone in the Buildings was common, but even there we were not as common as some.

After we had patted the horses, he bought me a glass of ginger beer to drink standing outside the pub with the mothers who had babies in prams, while he was inside with his mates.

Dad went to school long enough to learn to write (though he could never do his capitals properly) and to learn his tables, and that's all, but he had a way of being able to do sums in his head much quicker than anyone else could do them on paper. Joe said he had taught himself to do that so that he didn't get swindled by the bookies. Joe couldn't do it, nor could my uncle, even though he used to make fun of Dad most of the time.

When Dad was twelve years old, in 1901, he was put to work cleaning stables, and got on so well with the horses that they soon let him learn to drive them. He drove a big van like a furniture van, with a seat high up on the front, and he used to sit up in the air on his little seat, holding his whip and shouting "Below!" to people in the street to get out of the way. He did the same thing in the house sometimes, when he was carrying something and couldn't see in front of him. "Below!" he would shout, even if he was coming upstairs. It meant: Keep out of the way; I'm coming through.

When we lived in the Buildings he went to work six days a week, spent Saturday night at the pub, and on Sundays he mostly slept. He was always asleep when he wasn't working, although in Colliers Wood there was gardening to do, and wallpapering, and carpentry. Dad wouldn't do any of that. He mended our shoes—"snobbing," he called it—on an iron last that had four different-sized iron feet, but that was all.

"Other men build sheds, and grow potatoes and greens, and do all their own decorating. Why don't you?" Mum used to say, sort of getting at him.

Now he got noisy, to shut her up. "I wasn't brought up to it. None of us was in Lambeth, was we? I'm a good enough snob, but wallpapering's a trade, and I never learnt it. Now let me 'ave a few minutes bleeding peace by the fire, will you? I've been outside all day."

He spent the day either delivering frozen meat from the docks to Smithfield market for Lord Vestey ("He's spent his life making Lord Vestey rich," Uncle Ted said. "Haven't you, Jack?"), or moving furniture in his van around London. Dad's van had a secret compartment in the back where he kept things his family might need. Whenever we asked him for something, he always promised to have a look in the back of his van, and sometimes he would bring home what we wanted, a catapult, say, or a jigsaw puzzle. When I went with him to the stables on Sundays, I used to ask him to show me his van so I could have a look in the back, because there might be all kinds of things there that I did not know to ask for, but he always said the van was locked away on Sundays.

Sometimes, after a moving job, he found things in the back of his van for Mum, little things for the house like vases, and mantelpiece ornaments, and pictures. Most of these things Mum called "bloody rubbish," as if he couldn't be expected to know what was and what wasn't any good, although she kept them. But if it was something like a nice clock, she told him to take it back before the police came.

TWO

A Steamer to
Hampstead

MUM ALWAYS said she left home at fourteen, pushed out by her two brothers because the flat was getting too crowded as they all grew up. (Joe said she was actually seventeen, and the real reason she left was because she couldn't stand her own mother's slovenly ways. Grandma's hands, Joe said, were regularly as black as Newgate's knocker, even when she was cooking. But I think Mum is entitled to her own story.)

She never said where her mum came from but her dad was a Curnow, Matthew Curnow, which means his family came from Cornwall, donkey's years ago, Mum said. He worked for the gas company and at night he sang in pubs for drinks. He never told my grandma where he went at night, and she thought he might have been seeing his "fancy woman." One night, taking Mum with her, Gran tracked him down to the pub where he used to sing. As they walked into the music room, the emcee was announcing that Mister Matt Curnow would now sing "Look into My Eyes and Tell Me that You Love Me." My grandma stood up and said what she would do the next time Mister Matt Curnow looked into *her* eyes, and my grandad ran out the back door. When he came home, Grandma set about him until the police came to separate them.

Grandma couldn't stand the cold. When the wind got in the chimney she used to smash up a whole orange crate she got from the street market and stick it in the kitchen range all at once, shouting, "Burn, you bugger! Burn!" If the chimney caught fire, someone would bang on the door to tell her. "Mind your own bloody business," Grandma would shout at them, slamming the door. Then the police came, and then sometimes the fire brigade.

Grandma Curnow had a lot of Irish in her, Mum said. Sometimes the superintendent of the Buildings would knock on our door and tell us to take her in hand because she was dancing all round the square in her long black skirt, on her way to visit us. Round and round, she went, round and round. She often visited us in the afternoons when the pubs turned out.

When Mum was pushed out of her home, she found a room in a lodging house off Kennington Lane, two doors down from a knocking shop. Mum and Dad and Uncle Ted used to have a laugh about this on Saturday nights when they came back from the pub for some cold ham and pickles and thought the kids were all asleep. I asked our Ron what a knocking shop was. He didn't know but he thought it was probably a shop where people were always knocking stuff off, swiping it, nicking it, stealing, like. Mum said she and her landlady used to sit in their front window with the light off, spying on the men who knocked on the door of the shop.

She looked after herself by working for twelve hours a day in a Soho sweatshop. After that, she hated tailoring so much she never sewed up our clothes properly when we tore them. From the time I first noticed, most of the other kids at school had the holes in their clothes sewn over with neat little patches, but Mum sometimes didn't even bother to use the right colour thread on ours. "I've got no bloody time for all this," she would say. "Here, this will 'ave to do," as she sewed up a tear with big clumsy stitches. She never even tried to darn. I would see other kids' mums with a tennis ball in the heel of the sock they were mending, going over and under with the needle, over and under, until they had made a perfect patch, like trellis-work. The way Mum sewed it up, it made a blister in your heel. And yet, Gladys said, she was a tailoress, not just a seamstress. She could sew a whole suit with the tailor's help. But as far as mending *our* clothes was concerned, we were like the shoemaker's children.

When she lived in lodgings, before she married Dad, her landlady cooked her breakfast and her tea, and she bought a ha'p'orth of broken biscuits on the way to work for her dinner. In those days, grocers sold biscuits loose from big square tins, and sold off cheap the broken bits left in the bottom. She travelled to work in the West End by horse tram, which cost a ha'penny each way, so altogether she needed three ha'pence a day for her dinner and fares. But sometimes on Fridays, and even on Thursdays, she would be a ha'penny short, so she had to choose whether to go without her dinner or walk home over Westminster Bridge. Bloody miles it was, she used to say. On Saturdays she worked from eight in the morning until four in the afternoon, and this was called a half-day.

She was twenty when Dad became aware of her; he was two months younger. He still worked in the stables of the Union Cold Storage Company ("Lord Vestey's mob," he called it) and was just starting to be used sometimes as a driver. On Saturday nights he made a bit of extra money by helping out one or other of the street traders (usually the fish merchant) in Draper Street, off Newington Butts. The Draper Street market was the liveliest place to be on a Saturday night, all lit up with gas flares, crowded and noisy and friendly, and Mum often went there with a girlfriend to enjoy the crowds. Mum and Dad caught each other's eye, he winked at her when she passed by and she smiled back, and then one night he offered to buy her a bowl of eels and mash from the eel-and-pie shop after the market closed down. She had a friend with her, so he found a mate for her friend and the four of them went off to the shop where Dad proposed they have an outing together on bank holiday Monday. His mates at the stables went on outings on bank holidays, for a ride on a Thames steamer, or to the fair on Hampstead Heath. Dad put the two ideas together and said that a trip to the fair at Hampstead on a steamer might be a lark.

"You don't go to 'Ampstead on a steamer," Mum jeered. "Silly bugger. You go to 'Ampstead on a tram! 'Ampstead 'Eath's not on the water!"

Dad must have been "over the water" into London millions of times, moving people's furniture all over London, but he had never been on a bank holiday outing outside Lambeth. After Mum stopped laughing, she agreed to walk out with him on condition he give up selling fish in the market on Saturday nights. "I'm not," she said, "going out with a bloke who stands there, red in the face, shouting, ''Ere, 'oo wants a nice piece of 'addock?'"

So he gave up the fish barrow and got taken on full-time at the stables, and being, both, more or less on their own, it soon made sense for them to get married. She took him down to the pawnbroker, bought him his first suit and tie out of her savings, and they married and moved into two rooms in Penton Place.

Two rooms in Penton Place was all they could afford but it wasn't the slums, Mum used to say, don't get that idea. You white-stoned your front step every day and if you made too much noise, fighting and that, the police would come. Mum said the woman upstairs couldn't tell the time. "What time is it, Mrs. B.?" Mum would call up the stairs, teasing her, and Mrs. B. would call back, "It must be getting on, Mrs. Wright."

Every Wednesday Mrs. B. would pawn the waistcoat of her husband's Sunday suit for sixpence to buy herself a jug of beer, and if he suddenly wanted it before Friday, when she got her week's money, Mum would lend her the sixpence and the ha'penny interest. If her husband had found out what she was doing, he would have given her a good hiding, Mum said.

In my first clear memory of being separate from my mother, seeing her across the street or outside the school yard, and comparing her with other people's mothers (I was about six or seven), she was in her forties and had borne ten children, a middle-aged woman in a pinafore that crossed over itself and tied behind, with varicose veins and a complete set of false teeth. I have a photograph, which used to be on our mantelpiece, of her kneeling in a garden, dressed in a kimono and holding a fan in some photographer's idea of an artistic pose. The portrait shows her as a pretty young woman, and I think the Japanese gown, the fan, the screens, for all that they are part of the studio's wardrobe, represent her desire to see herself in some better light than any her own daylight world could provide. There was one flaw: in the picture her mouth is closed. She had lost all her teeth by the time she was twenty-one for lack of even minimal attention, a common enough plight in Lambeth at the time, and even later. When the picture was taken she was keeping the decay out of sight.

My father still had three teeth when I began to notice him, enough to serve him for another ten years. The English are no longer notorious for their teeth, and for the enormous amounts of sweets children used to consume (although, as I write this there is a report in a Toronto newspaper that every man, woman, and child in England is still eating three-quarters of a pound of sweets and chocolate a week, the highest per capita consumption in Europe). Until the war, though, the addiction to sweets was such that a thriller writer—I think Eric Ambler—used the bad condition of a murder victim's teeth as a clue to his national identity. My generation was saved by the war, when sweets were rationed. And we got our teeth examined at school (usually on the day we were inspected for lice) and the bad ones pulled, a fairly rudimentary treatment, but enough along with the promotion in the schools of the idea of brushing teeth, to make sure that there would not be nearly so many children with rotting teeth in the future.

It is clear from the photograph of my mother, and the record of her later achievements, that my father was lucky to get her. For other reasons, my mother was lucky to get him. She must have been very anxious to secure a beachhead on the shores of respectability, to establish residence there, and to do that she needed access to the wages of a man who worked regularly, didn't drink much, kept his betting within bounds, and who would let her manage their life together, and for all this my father was the answer. He wanted her; she wanted what he could provide: it was a fair bargain.

Next to her picture on the mantelpiece was a picture of them together, her sitting in a chair holding her first baby, Violet, him standing beside her in the suit he was married in. She used to show people where she had pencilled in his hair because he was bald when they got married, which he said was caused by carrying heavy weights on his head. It is the only picture of them that has survived.

Dad spent the war years in France in the Durham Light Infantry. He had no connection with the county of Durham, but the army was already beginning to mix up its recruits to avoid having whole villages and towns depleted of their young men after a battle. Dad spent some time in the trenches, but for most of the war he was an ostler, looking after the regiment's horses. He hardly ever mentioned the war, and the only effect on him, as far as I could tell, was that he became fanatical about the importance of well-polished shoes. He wouldn't take us kids out unless our shoes were gleaming with polish, including the instep underneath.

In 1918 Dad came back from the war and went back to the stables. He was now a proper full-time carter and sometimes he was away for a week at a time as he took his four horses and his van on a long road trip. They were still living in Penton Place, but now Mum set about getting ready for the first move.

When she had six children, the family qualified by the rules of the Guinness Trust for a flat in the Buildings, where we lived until there were too many of us. As each one left school at fourteen, my mother found them respectable jobs and took back most of their wages for housekeeping. (She used to go down to Kennington Cross on Friday nights to meet Dad when he got his pay packet, so that he wouldn't do anything silly like spending her housekeeping money.) Three girls were apprenticed to tailors, because, Mum said, although it was a hard life it was dependable, with good earnings and steady employment, although Lil couldn't get on with it and became a waitress, a "Nippie," in a Lyons teashop. Just as well, Lil used to say; if she had stayed in tailoring, she might not have met Sid, and clicked.

Mum found Joe a nice clean job as a clerk in Crosse and Blackwell's, so with the first four kids and my Dad all bringing in wages, and still eleven of us at home, Mum decided it was time to move from the Buildings. Besides, she'd always fancied herself in a house of her own one day, one with a garden to sit out in on a hot day.

It had to be somewhere on the Northern Line so that Dad could get to his stables and the girls could get to work in the West End. Mum had never been anywhere south of Stockwell, so whenever she got the chance she went for a ride on the Northern Line to have a look round. As far south as Tooting it was still old London, but at the next stop on the line, Colliers Wood, there were some nice housing estates, and she found a house to let on one of them, not far from the shops, and only two streets away from the tube. So we moved out to Colliers Wood.

Once upon a time there were charcoal burners in Colliers Wood, but they were long gone, and only the name was left. Now it was just a stop on the Northern Line, but it was a nicer place for the girls to bring their young men home to than the Buildings. Dad never got used to it. He couldn't walk to his stables any more; he had to catch the first train up in the morning (long before the clerks left for the City), dressed in winter in a big mackintosh coat under which he wore a woollen cardigan and a waistcoat, with a scarf knotted at the neck and a cap. And after being perched up on his seat on the van all day long in the pouring rain, he had a long ride home on the Underground in wet clothes, smelling of horses. When he got home, he ate his tea in the kitchen, sat in front of the fire for an hour, and went to bed with a couple of the old overcoats which hung behind the kitchen door, piled on top of his blankets. What he liked best was a mug of tea with two spoonfuls of tinned milk and two spoons of sugar, in front of a roaring fire. He could, Mum said, burn a hundredweight of coal if you didn't watch him; it was by watching him, and the coal, and the food bill, and everything else, that she had been able to bring us to Colliers Wood and take us for a week's holiday at the seaside every year.

Dad didn't seem like the rest of us; more like a lodger, really. To me, he was a bit of a stranger, someone who ate in the kitchen with the door shut because he liked kippers and fried bloaters which filled the room with blue, fishy smoke, and who washed in the kitchen, too, because it was warm and he liked the big stone sink to wash in. I saw him wash once or twice, not often, because he was very shy. He stripped to the waist, covered his chest and arms and shoulders, as well as his face and neck, with soap, and rubbed himself like a madman, blowing hard all the time. Mum used to tell him not to make such a bloody performance out of washing—she was always chattering on at him not to do this or that—but Joe said it was a habit he got into from trying not to breathe in the chaff when he was rubbing down horses, an ostler's habit. Like shouting "Below!" when anyone got in his way when he was carrying something, as if he was perched up on his van, shouting down to the street. Joe said Dad got most of his other habits from the war. After four years in France he had learned what he needed for his comfort. He washed himself in nearly boiling water because he never knew when he might find hot water again, scrubbing away with the yellow soap like someone who found being clean a luxury. It was from his hatred of the cold in the trenches that he developed a passion for a roaring fire, and the tea he drank, thick and sweet, was the kind he had learned to like in the army. And whenever he got a day off he took to his bed and slept, at least all afternoon, because he said he didn't think he would ever get caught up.

What I could never get over from seeing him washing himself was the size of his chest and arms, because I always thought that since he was short he must be little. But, of course, he spent all morning lifting sides of beef on and off his van. Joe told me that before he was married he used to be a sparring partner in an illegal bare-knuckles ring in Blackfriars, but Mum made him give it up. He never hit anybody in our house, including me, even when Mum asked him to, which was just as well because he had big, horny hands from lifting things and from handling the reins. You would have known it if he *had* hit you. But he wasn't like that. My sister remembers him as the one who stayed with her when the fever wagon came when she had scarlet fever and held her hand all the way to the hospital, saying, "You'll be all right, duck," over and over again, until the nurse took over, making himself late for work and nearly losing his job.

I only saw him lose his temper once. Mum had gone too far: she was nagging him while he was eating his tea, telling him not to make so much noise, chewing. He put down his knife and fork and said, "Am I going to have my tea in peace, or not?" Whatever she said next was too much. He opened the kitchen door, threw his kipper into the garden, plate as well, put on some coats, and marched to the front door.

"Where do you think you're going?" Mum cried, a bit afraid.

"Aht," he said and slammed the door. When he came back, about two hours later, he had drunk a few pints, a thing he never did during the week, and he went back to his place in the kitchen and sat down.

"There's no more kippers if that's what you're looking for," Mum said, still trying to win but a bit fearful of the way he was acting.

"Bacon sandwich will do," he said, and waited.

She grumbled all the time she was frying it, but he got his bacon sandwich and went to bed.

He knew London inside out, so he was always being asked directions. One of us would say, "How do I get to the War Museum, Dad?" and he'd come back right away, "Go-to-the-Elephant-on-the-tube-and-walk-back-along-St.-George's," all in a single mouthful because, given the chance, someone else might offer directions and there would be an argument because one of the very few things he got upset about was when someone tried to correct him on directions. He was very proud of his knowledge of directions. "Are you sitting there, trying to tell me 'ow to get to London Bridge from Lambeth Palace, me, who've drove that bleedin' route with a van and four horses, rain and shine, for thirty years? Now listen to what I'm saying, and don't interrupt." But except for getting directions, no one took much notice of him.

Sometimes he came home from the stables with stories he had got from his mates, and Mum laughed at him for believing such tommy-rot. One of his mates told him that all the tarts in Piccadilly, over the water, were French. No English girl would do that, his mate told him, but French girls had no morals whatsoever. Dad had grown up not far from the Waterloo Road where the English girls plied their trade, and he had spent four years in France during the war, and he must have known as much about it as they did, but he didn't *know* he knew it because it was still always "My mate at work claims . . ." and my mother would interrupt with, "Don't you 'ave anything better to do in those stables than sit about talking bloody rubbish." Once, lying in bed in the dark on a Saturday night after they had all come back from the pub and were talking downstairs, I heard my uncle tell the story of how Dad, during the war, was given charge of a dozen horses with orders to move them back some miles behind the lines. "He lost the lot," Uncle Ted said. "Didn't you, Jack? One by one, they were all killed by enemy action, that right, Jack? And they believed him. Believed every word. That right, Jack? You could get anything you wanted for the price of a cart horse, right, Jack? Mam'selle from Armentières, parley-vous, eh, Jack?"

"That's enough," Mum said.

"More than enough, I should think. Eh, Jack? Still, you never knew if it might be the last, eh, Jack?"

Mostly Dad lived apart from us, and as long as he got his meals he allowed Mum to nag him about his table manners and his grammar. She did stop him changing his *v*'s for *w*'s. As Mum told the story, by the time they were married, no one who knew any better was doing it, and those who did, like Dad, did it deliberately to show where they came from. Occasionally, when Mum wasn't listening, he would try a phrase in the old way. "Be wery partic'ler about your boots," he might say. "Bloke with wet feet is in trouble from the start." But she couldn't stop him using rhyming slang which came as naturally to him as breathing, and we often had to ask him what he meant. One he used a lot was "Kate," as in, "When I was in the Kate," meaning *army*, from the rhyme with Kate Carney, a famous music hall comedienne.

After we moved to Colliers Wood and I was allowed to play on the street, I dodged him in public. We had nothing to say if I saw him coming home from work, and besides, it was embarrassing when he called me by one of my brothers' names in front of my mates. He knew I belonged to him but he was not always sure which one I was. Once, when it was getting dark, our gang of six-year-olds was lined up under a street light comparing dicks when I heard my dad's voice from across the street. The dark was thick beyond the gaslight and we did not realize anyone could see us. "You dirty little buggers," he shouted. "Stop that or I'll tell your fathers, the lot of you."

We ran like hell, and I spent the next half-hour in terror, wondering what would happen to me. I knew that what we were doing was dirty in some way, and I had no idea what he would do to me for it, even though he had never hit me for anything else. When the fear of what my mum would do to me for staying out past my bedtime was greater than the fear of my dad, I slunk back home and let myself in the back door, right into the kitchen where he was eating his kippers.

"Close the door, Len," he said. "It's cold."

And that was all. The shouting hadn't meant anything. I worshipped him for a week after that, for not telling my mum. It was my mate Robbie who said he probably hadn't recognized me.

He wouldn't have any dirty talk in the house. There was a time, years after this, during the war, when the BBC was beginning to warn about venereal diseases, and he would rush to the wireless and switch it off when the subject cropped up. The station that really bothered him, though, was the American Armed Forces Network, which I had on a lot because it played Glen Miller, endlessly. It used to sign off with a warning, something like, "Blindness! Madness! Limbs drop off! Watch out, fellas! That's VD!" Followed by "The Stars and Stripes Forever."

Three

The Crystal Palace

I WAS the ninth, and none of my pals came from families as big as mine. For years I overheard people wondering about the obvious question: How was it that a woman like my mother allowed herself to become pregnant every two years for twenty years? The only comment I ever heard by way of answer was one she made when my sister told her she had no intention of having more than three children. "It's not up to you, is it?" Mum reminded her. My sister disagreed and got the courage to ask her why she didn't, at some point, take charge of the situation. Mum said that Dad wouldn't take no for an answer, his grounds being that it was well known that the denial of rights was one of the causes of consumption, the most dreaded disease of the day. His mates in the stable had told him this.

Once a year, when my dad brought his van and horses home, I became proud of my dad. Other kids boasted about what their dads did, but none of them had a father who parked a giant green and gold pantechnicon and four huge gleaming horses outside the house while he ate his midday dinner. Which brings me to Robbie.

Some of the other kids I played with on the street were from families like ours, born in Lambeth or Brixton or Camberwell and moved out to the suburbs like us when they saw their chance to get a better place to live. The family next door to us followed us to Colliers Wood from the Buildings. Not that we had much to do with each other as neighbours, and no one hardly ever invited a neighbour inside, because in Colwood Gardens people judged you by the way you lived more than they did in the Buildings. No one hardly ever invited a neighbour inside in case they sized you up, judged if you were a bit common. In the Buildings you had to be a bit common to qualify for a flat so there was no point in putting on airs.

My mum drummed it into us that when we went out we were never to talk about the way we lived indoors. Once my sister heard me telling the boy next door that in our family you got three slices of bread and margarine for breakfast, a hot dinner at noon, and three slices of bread and margarine and a slice of cake at night, all washed down with tea.

"We can have as many slices as we like," he lied. I knew for a fact that some mornings he went to school on a single piece of fried bread. My sister heard me talking while she was skipping rope and told my mother, who shouted at me for telling everyone our business. Of course, what she was afraid of was that one of us would complain of being hungry outside the house. Before the war we were always slightly hungry. There was no food to spare, and we were never allowed to help ourselves, not even to bread and jam. After their Saturday night suppers, there would sometimes be leftovers in the larder, and early on Sunday morning you could steal a slice of cheese or a piece of cake so that it might not be noticed, but that was all.

My mother had nothing to fear from us. We knew what shame was from a very early age, and accepted our share of the task of keeping up a family front, as did many of the kids I knew. The one exception, the outsider to our status-conscious world, was Robbie. He was a local kid, not an immigrant from Lambeth or Camberwell. His family had lived in Colliers Wood since before it was built over, when it was in the country almost, and they still lived in one of a row of houses that had been built before the First World War. Robbie said they had once lived in a tied cottage but I don't know what it would have been tied to. They had gaslight in his house like we used to have in the Buildings, though Colwood Gardens was all electric. Robbie's father worked in the fields for a market gardener, and when he cycled down Colwood Gardens on his way home at the end of the day he always had some carrots, or onions, or some runner beans on the carrier behind him. He had an allotment, too, where he grew his own vegetables, over in Mitcham where there were still fields. Robbie's kitchen was the only one open to the rest of us on a rainy day—his mother was away, working as a cook in a lunatic asylum—and it was warm, and jolly, and furnished with things like rocking chairs that went back more generations than the rest of us had. Robbie's family never put on airs; they brought home enough money and stuff from the father's allotment to fill the house with food, and that's all they wanted. And they had a big black kitchen range that kept the room as snug as a bakery, instead of a posh tiled fireplace that didn't draw properly like the houses on Colwood Gardens. On a winter's night Robbie's family toasted themselves pink while the rest of us huddled around our fireplaces, trying to economize on coal. (In our house, if the coal actually glowed, then it was "damped down" with a soggy bundle of potato peelings wrapped in newspaper to make it burn slower.)

So Robbie was an outsider, and though he was my mate, he never joined the street gang that I was part of. He was born in Mitcham, and his uncles still worked as agricultural labourers on the smallholdings that were left, like his dad, and though he and I became mates, he never joined in the street games of football and such. He didn't like rules, and he didn't like having a captain over him, so when I joined in these games he sloped off. Mothers didn't trust him because they could smell that he might lead their kids into trouble; he didn't seem to have the same respect for adults that had been drummed into the rest of us and mothers warned their kids not to play with him. A lot of the kids themselves felt his difference from them and were wary of him, as if he were black or a gypsy.

Robbie knew all about the district we lived in; he belonged there and had cousins nearby, whereas the rest of us had left our relatives behind in Kennington. He knew from his family who owned the big houses, and he was good on history. He knew when the last lavender fields in Mitcham had been worked, and what Colwood Gardens was like before our houses had been built, and he knew the story of Merton Abbey—the ruins were nearby—and Lord Nelson, who met his girlfriend in a house in Merton, and why the bit of land at the end of Colwood Gardens was called the Pickle: his dad said it was originally the Pike Hole, where the monks from Merton Abbey stored their fish.

Once Robbie took me off to visit another gang a mile away, in the old part of Mitcham down Church Road, a gang of nine-year-olds whose leader was a cousin of Robbie's, a boy who had no bone in his little finger, and who could talk to the gypsies who lived on Western Road. This gang had a sort of clubhouse, an old yellow wooden house that stood on its own in a field past Phipp's Bridge. No one still lived in it but it belonged to an old man who kept chasing them off. One day he called the police, but they never caught any of the gang. A few days later the house caught fire and burned to the ground. Robbie said his cousin had done it because the old man set the police on them.

Robbie knew a lot of places beyond the streets where we played, the common land, and the wild places. He showed me where to catch newts in the River Wandle behind the box factory, and he knew the best places for scrumping apples. My mum didn't actually stop me playing with him, but she also thought he might have a bit of gypsy in him, and she didn't like to see me too thick with him.

The difference between Robbie's world and mine showed up during a "dare," which Robbie liked to do. You could dare him to do anything that was possible. His dad said you could dare him to eat shit if you would fry it. Robbie liked anything fried. This time the dare involved Robbie, me, and a girl who would take her knickers off if you would, too. We did it in the nightwatchman's hut on a building site, and the knickers were just coming down when Robbie shouted a warning. There, moving across the site from the street, was a copper. This time I ran clear into the next postal district with Robbie behind me, laughing his head off, and the copper shouting, "I saw you. I'll be round to your father tonight."

When we had outrun him I was still hysterical. "What am I going to do?" I cried. "He'll tell my mum."

Robbie was still laughing. "He won't come rahnd," he said. "If he does, he won't know you. Tell him it was me. My mum don't care."

What kind of family did he come from that his mum didn't care about him doing dirty stuff?

Robbie was the only one of my mates who admired my dad. Some of my other new mates, the sons of the clerks in bowler hats, had picked up from their families that my dad was inferior to theirs, but by the time Robbie was nine years old he didn't care what the other kids' mothers thought, especially the ones who had warned their kids against him, and also the fathers who could smell the outsider in him as well as his potential for making fun of them. They got snotty when he called round. Robbie didn't knock at the door and ask nicely, "Is Wallie or Alec home?" He shouted "Wally!" up at the house from the street, and grown-ups often told him to stop shouting and go away, back to "your own street." He lived on Clarendon Road among people like himself, they thought, people with no manners.

My dad liked him, though. He called him "a proper little tyke" and knew his name when he forgot mine. Robbie liked the rich, horsey smell of my dad and the fact that he didn't wear a tie. "'Allo, Mr. Wright," Robbie would shout from across the street when he saw my dad. "'Allo, you young bugger," my dad would shout back. "What you up to, then?"

Once a year my dad showed his horses at the Crystal Palace, the glass-and-iron pavilion put up for the Great Exhibition of 1851, where prizes were awarded every year, until it burned down, prizes in the form of horse brasses for the best turned-out horses and carts. My dad groomed his four horses until they shone, and washed his van, and walked the team the five or seven miles from the stables to our house where he ate his dinner before he put on a clean cap and went on to the exhibition. Even after the Crystal Palace burned down, they still had a show of the horses and carts.

Dad parked outside our house for an hour, four huge horses with feet the size of manhole covers, hooked up to his giant green van. He hung feed bags on them and went in to his dinner. The horses were as quiet as lambs, so there was no need to watch them. I always hung about, though, pretending to mind them while my dad ate his dinner, and Robbie patted them and ran home to get carrots to feed them. The other kids all kept back.

And then, one day, something frightened one of the horses and it tried to rear, and suddenly it was as terrifying to a kid as seeing two fathers fighting outside a pub on a Sunday. The lead horse was plunging up and down in his traces, rearing right up and then smashing his feet on the ground, and the other three were trying to get away from him. But there was nowhere for them to run in Colwood Gardens, and if they really bolted, they would smash into everything on the street. I ran inside shouting for my dad, "Come quick, come quick, the 'orses are bolting." My mum said, "I knew this would happen if you brought those bloody 'orses 'ome."

When he came out, the street was empty as the mothers shouted for their children to come away, all except for Robbie who was dancing about in front of the horses, shouting "Whoa!" and laughing. Robbie and I watched, then, as my dad caught the reins on the lead horse as it plunged out of the sky and, so it looked to us, settled it down with one blow. He just punched the horse on the nose, and it stopped leaping and stood quivering, and the others quietened down, too.

"That's my dad," I said to a clerk who was standing in his doorway, watching the excitement.

When the horses had settled down, my dad looked at me and Robbie in turn. "One of you go up on top," he said. "Tighten the reins. The other one stand in front like you was doing, young fella. They won't go anywhere if they see you in the way."

Robbie and I looked at each other. The choice was mine—he was *my* dad—and I looked up at the driver's seat, a narrow wooden bench that looked as high up as a house roof. I could see Robbie was dying to go up. "I'll go," I said, and I climbed the iron rungs on the side of the van all the way up to the little seat just under the top of the van. I didn't try to tighten the reins, just clamped my hands around them and the iron bar they were knotted to. My dad went back and finished his dinner.

I sat there for about ten minutes. Far below on the street, Robbie stroked the lead horse and grinned up at me. After a bit, I grinned back. All round us the other kids, and some of the adults, were keeping their distance. Soon my dad came out of the house, buttoning his coats.

"Right," he said to me. "You want to come to the 'orse show?"

My mum was standing in the doorway, but not interfering, so I could go if I wanted. I nodded.

He turned to Robbie. "What abaht you, young 'un?"

"He'll have to go home and ask his mum," my mum said, from the doorway.

Robbie called out, "My mum won't mind," and climbed up the side of the van like a monkey and sat beside me, grinning his head off.

My dad climbed up after Robbie—there was just room for three of us on the seat—shook up the reins, shouted out the drayman's warning, "Below," and we sailed off, clattering and jingling. My mum called out something from the door of the house, some kind of warning. My dad waved his whip at her. "Don't take any notice of 'er," he said to me. "You're wiv me now."

Four

Excursions

PLAYING ON the streets was all right after school and Saturday afternoons, but on Sundays and bank holidays we wanted to explore, and for that we needed at least a common. Mitcham was the closest common, but we didn't use it much. Mitcham Common was covered in gorse bushes, and full of boggy patches, with hardly any trees and no real secret places. We caught frogs on Mitcham Common, and went to the Mitcham Fair on August bank holiday Mondays, but for a real day out we went to Wimbledon Common which had woods and ferns and pine needles and acorns, and even conkers. You could get lost on Wimbledon Common; it was the sort of place where Robin Hood hid out when the Sheriff of Nottingham was after him. Robbie said that was why one of the roads was called Robin Hood Lane.

We took the number 2 or 4 tram from Colliers Wood to Wimbledon station, riding upstairs in the front—it felt like being on a steamboat—and walked up the hill through the village to the common. All afternoon we played: Robbie was Robin Hood, of course, and I was Friar Tuck, because I admired Friar Tuck's quarterstaff, the one he knocked Robin Hood into the river with, above all other weapons. Robbie could beat me, and everybody else of the same weight, at wrestling, hitting, running, cycling, swimming, throwing stones, distance spitting, conkers, the catapult, and the peashooter, but until we tested them, until we actually had got hold of two six-to-eight-foot staves to see, I kept my belief that I would beat him at quarterstaff.

So we roamed through Sherwood Forest on sunny afternoons, often lost—me, not Robbie—looking for burrows, finding small dead animals and birds, carving our initials on the trees with his penknife, until, tired and dusty, in the shank of the afternoon, it was time to go to the Windmill and spend our last tuppence on an ice-cream cone. Then Robbie said, "Sh-sh-sh," and we crawled silently through the undergrowth, single file—stalking the Sheriff of Nottingham—when Robbie dropped to his belly and we slithered to a place in the grass, a little rise that overlooked a bosky dell, and there they were, his grey flannel bum going up and down, up and down, and her holding the box of chocolates up to the light so she could see to pick out the ones with the soft centres. They'd taken their shoes off, but nothing else.

It was all new to me but I had a sense we were playing forbidden games: a sense that if he saw us, he would kill us.

"Run!" I whispered.

"Sh-sh-sh!"

He showed me a handful of acorns, and lobbed one into the dell.

Missed. He threw another, this time bouncing it off the left cheek. The bum kept going, not feeling the acorn through the flannel, but Frankie's next acorn landed in her chocolates and she looked up and saw us and screamed and he jumped up, and then we ran, but not hard because he couldn't chase us like that.

As soon as we came to a regular footpath, thick with people taking their Sunday constitutionals on the common, a lot of the girls holding the little black books they took to church, Robbie stopped so that he could laugh in comfort. "He won't chase us this far," he said. "Not wiv just his socks on."

"What were they doing?"

"'Aving a go."

"What?"

"Making a baby."

"How?"

"You saw."

"Yeah, but how?"

"He put his winkle in her."

"In where she widdles from?"

Robbie had no sisters. He shook his head. "They have two," he said. "One for widdling and one for doing that. You have to do that if you want a baby. Your mum and dad did that to get you."

I hit him then, and went on hitting him while he danced around me, naming all the people I liked, including Deanna Durbin, who did it all the time. I ran off and went home on my own. When I got home I asked my mum how babies really got started. "Oh, Gawd 'elp us, *I* don't know," she said, flustered but laughing a little. "Ask your mates. They'll know."

The Vogue Cinema, Tooting Broadway, was a fleapit which showed not-too-old pictures for half the price of the Odeon or the Granada. We used to go there on Saturday afternoons. The program usually included a Will Hay comedy about a schoolmaster who ran a school for dunces. One week the main feature was *Beau Geste*, which we sat through twice by hiding in the toilet between shows.

Beau Geste is a story about three English brothers, members of the upper-class Geste family, played by Gary Cooper, Ray Milland, and Robert Preston, who join the Foreign Legion to save the family honour when a family jewel is stolen. The Foreign Legion stuff was fine, all about Arabs attacking the fort which two of the Geste brothers were helping to defend, and how the legionnaires got killed off one by one until only one brother is left, but the scene which we really stayed for was the naval battle in which the three brothers as children destroy two marvellous model galleons in order to have a toy Viking funeral. The scene is a foreshadowing of the final scene in the desert— even at ten we could feel that—but we didn't care about the story. It was the ships we cared about. We could not imagine a world in which not only did such toys exist—each of the ships must have cost six months of my dad's wages—but that playing with them included setting them on fire. What other toys did they set fire to? Did they do this every Saturday afternoon?

And then, at the climax of the naval battle scene, a visitor appears, a major from the Foreign Legion (part of the foreshadowing thing), just after one of the boys has been shot in the leg with a toy cannonball as he is wading in the pond after the galleons, and the eldest boy, played by Donald O'Connor, has dug it out with his penknife. As the major was congratulating Donald O'Connor for his skill as a surgeon, Robbie jumped up and shouted, "Dad! Dad!" at the top of his voice.

Everybody round us started shouting to tell him to sit down and shut up, which he quickly did.

"What's the matter with you?" I whispered, trying to bring him to his senses. "You having a fit? Your dad's not here!"

"I know. But the old bloke sitting next to me was trying to get my dick out and that was the best way I could think of to make him stop. Did you see him run?"

"Why was he trying to do that?"

"They do that, some old men. My dad said if anyone asks me to show them my dick, to shout out, wherever I am. Worked, didn't it?"

"But what did he want to get your dick out for?"

Robbie thought for a moment. "He wanted to cut it off. That's it. They want to cut them off."

That made sense. It was already the most interesting and valuable part of me: it made sense that out there in the dark there were creatures looking to cut it off.

The world faded at Tooting Broadway to the north and Wimbledon Common to the south. We made excursions by bike to the Thames at Hampton Court on holidays, to fish from the towpath and swim in water the colour of strong tea, but mainly our world was the streets, most of all the corner of Colwood Gardens and Clarendon Road. Where the two streets joined, the last house on Clarendon Road was finished off with a blank wall, ideal for marking in chalk a football goal, or three cricket stumps, or just throwing a ball against and calling the name of the kid who had to catch it or run the gauntlet. The games ended when the man of the house, sick of the thump, thump, thump against his ear while he was trying to listen to the wireless inside, came roaring out of the front door and grabbed the ball and took it inside.

We would wait for a few minutes and then Robbie would knock on the door and ask for our ball back.

"I've chucked it on the fire," the man would say. "Now, sod off, the lot of you."

"There's no smoke coming out your chimney," Robbie would say. "Come on, mister, gi's our ball."

"I'll set the bleedin' dog on you. Now bugger off."

Robbie would run home then and come back with his mum.

She would stand at the gate while Robbie knocked on the door again, ready to march up the garden path. When the door opened, she shouted, "Wasssermatterwivyou? Don't you like kids? Spoiling their little games. Give them their ball or I'll come in there and get it myself."

He was no match for Robbie's mum; he always gave in, usually by throwing the ball out the door just as he slammed it shut. Then Robbie's mum turned on us. "Now listen to me, you lot. If I hear any more about your bloody ball, I'll throw it down the drain, I will. And I'll tan *your* arse, Robbie. So go 'ome, the lot of you. Or go and play in the rec. That's what it's for."

But the recreation ground was a no man's land; strange kids from other streets used the rec; you couldn't trust them not to gang up on you, and tie you up to a tree and make you eat earwigs and worms. No, the corner of Colwood Gardens and Clarendon Road was where we belonged, and it belonged to us. We were safe there.

Once a year there was another world—the seaside.

We usually went to Sheerness. Southend was nearer and easier to get to but because of that my mum thought it attracted a rougher type of person. Along the front at Southend, behind the rail overlooking the beach, a row of deckchairs belonged by right to mothers from the East End, dressed, from the point of view of kids on the beach below, in giant bloomers of green or pink or sky blue underneath skirts pulled up so their knees could catch the sun, real "gorblimeys," my mum called them, who shouted jokes at each other.

"'Ow's your belly orf for spots, then, Maisie?" This was a way of saying hello, not a real question.

"Same's yours, Em. Same's yours."

"You're in a bad way, then, Maisie."

"'Oo ain't, Em? 'Oo ain't? No use complaining about it, though, is there?"

Then a male voice from the row of deckchairs behind: "Shut up, Maisie, for Gawd's sake. You're *outside* now."

"Shut up, yourself, bleedin' misery. Read your paper. You orf, Em? Cheerio, then. Mind 'ow you go."

That was what my mum meant by common. Common as dirt.

So we went to Sheerness, across the river from Southend, and sometimes to Ramsgate around the coast, or to Margate.

My mum kept her money—our money—in a leather purse with about seven compartments like a concertina, each compartment reserved for a different budget: food, coals, savings for a new settee, shillings for the gas and electricity meters (never put in in time to avoid the sudden plunge into darkness and the lengthy fumble in the cupboard under the stairs, feeling for the slot of the meter), holidays, and co-op checks, imitation coins that came with the groceries and were saved to be exchanged one day for "dividends" to be spent on merchandise. All our coals were paid for with co-op dividends, as well as the kids' clothes.

All year she fed coins into the holiday compartment of her purse, coins that turned into ten-shilling notes, then pound notes, which were then moved to the back of the purse underneath two leather crossstraps for safety. Early in the year she wrote the letter.

Dear Madam,
Re your advert in *Dalton's Weekly*. Require accommodation for week of July 3 to 10. Husband, wife, and six children under fourteen. [The older girls were by now going on their own holidays.] Cooking attendance required.

And oblige,
(Mrs.) C. A. Wright

"Cooking attendance" meant that the landlady would cook what the guests brought, but would not supply meals; a form of self-catering. I don't know where she picked up "and oblige."

We travelled usually by train, taking turns to put our heads out the window to see the tunnels coming.

"When the man on the train asks you for your ticket, don't forget, you're not five yet."

"But I am, I'm six and a half."

"No you're not, not on the train, and don't you forget."

We changed at Sittingbourne, and once, on the platform of the Sittingbourne station while we were waiting for the train to Sheerness, a woman in a big hat offered to buy Doris, whose dark curly ringlets had taken her fancy. Seeing so many kids in one family, the woman thought she would be relieving my mother of some of her burden by giving Doris a good home.

"*Buy her?*" my mother shouted. "*Buy* one of my kids? You cheeky bitch. You bloody cow. You saying my kids don't have a good home? I know your kind. You want a toy, you do. You'll bring her back when you're tired of her. Ask your 'usband to give you one, if you've got a 'usband, that is. Bloody cheek. Too good to have your own, are you? Sauce. Go on. Leave us alone. Go on. You and your money. Sod off."

When we went to Ramsgate, we took the charabanc from Victoria. Once, a mate of my dad's offered to take us all in his taxi for less than all our fares by train, on the understanding that dad would get out and walk when they came to any hills to cut down the weight.

They packed the clothes for all eight of us in one big old suitcase which expanded nearly to the size we needed, then bulged to make room for the rest. My dad had to sit on it to get it to click shut, then strap it up with a leather belt he brought from his stables, and finally lash it with a rope to make a handle because the original handle had torn out its fastenings the first time dad had tried to lift it packed. My mum complained it was a bloody disgrace, but the only alternative was the kitbag my dad had brought back from the Great War. She packed a shopping bag full of cheese-and-tomato sandwiches and cake, and one bar of chocolate each, relying on being able to buy cups of tea at stops along the way. In spite of all the warnings—"Eat it now, Greedy-Guts, and there'll be no more"—we clamoured for our choco-late immediately, so it was all gone before we left London, because anyone who tried to hang on to it found themselves sharing what was rightfully all theirs. You didn't *have* to share, but there were too many risks involved in being a sole possessor. ("Give Jean a bit of yours, there's a duck, she dropped hers on the floor.")

In the boarding house we found a room full of beds, smelling of seaweed and Sunlight soap, with sheets hard and smooth, where we woke up to the smell of the sea. But no one could get up until Mum said we could.

Breakfast was porridge, bread and jam, and tea. Then all day on the beach with the rest of Lambeth. Sandwiches of cheese, tomato, lettuce, and sand, an orange each, and a bag of chips between two, different from the chips at home, bigger, fried with their skins on and sold in a paper bag like an army forage cup upside down. Mum and Dad bought cups of tea; at one time, Mum said, you could carry down your own teapot and buy hot water from a cottage at the end of the beach, but it was easier just to buy a cup of tea when you wanted it. Mum gave us enough pennies for two goes each day on one of the machines on the pier; we spent the rest of the day on the sand, building castles, paddling, getting burnt. One year Len came out in blisters all over his back and we had to find a nurse.

Then dragging home at the end of the day, nearly dead from the sun, back to the boarding house with a piece of smoked haddock to be cooked for tea, bought from the fish shop which advertised FISH: WET, DRIED, AND FRIED. Sometimes for a treat we would get a poached egg on top, with cake for afters. Then bed.

"But, Mum, it's broad daylight!"

At home, in summer, we played on the street until dusk, nine o'clock at least.

"I know what time it is. Now get to bed. You've 'ad your day, now we're 'aving ours. This is *my* 'oliday, too, mine and Dad's."

Their holiday was a walk along the front without us, ending in a pint of mild and a glass of Guinness in the pub on the corner.

We settle down to a game of I Spy, knowing we'll be awake for ever, warned about making any noise. The landlady offers to listen for us. "You go orf and enjoy yourselves, Mrs. Wright. They'll be all right."

We are asleep before they are out the door.

Every day begins with a walk to a different part of the beach before we make camp, comparing. "I like it away from the pier best, not so many people walking all over you when you're trying to 'ave a picnic."

"It's hard to find a place where you can get a cup of tea if you go too far that way."

"I wouldn't mind a walk round Sheerness this afternoon, so let's stay near the pier."

"Ah, Mum, can we stay on the beach? There's nothing to do in Sheerness."

"No, you can't. You'll end up drowned. I know you."

"Leave them be, Daisy. I'll look after them."

"Mind you keep your eye on them, then. And Jack, don't be buying them packets and packets of sweets, you hear? One stick of rock each is plenty."

It never rained.

Then home on Saturday, finding Joe, who had been left behind to look after himself for the first time in his life because he had a job and his week's holiday didn't fit in with ours, caught in the side-splitting act of loading the copper with all the cups and saucers and plates he had used all week, preparing to boil them all up before we got back. He'd never done the washing-up before, not with Mum and three grown-up sisters.

Then out on the street to show off the sunburn to kids whose families never bothered with holidays. Not everybody's mother had a purse like ours.

Five

Diversions

MY DAD was glad to be home. He was a betting man, and it was hard to find a bookie in a strange town, so a week at the seaside was like a week of Sundays to him, with nothing to look forward to. In our house, bets were sent off every day written out on scraps of paper in indelible pencil, wrapped around the coins that were being bet. Sometimes, when I had learned proper handwriting, Dad got me to write them out.

1 s. Each Way, Laughing Boy (three o'clock Sandown) A.T.C.
1 s. Each Way, Black Jack (3:20 Ascot)

That is, a shilling to win and a shilling to place (in the first three), on the three o'clock race at Sandown Park. A.T.C. meant "any to come" (any winnings) to be made into another each-way bet on the 3:20 at Ascot. A double was a bet on one race, which if won, was then bet on another. Doubles, trebles, accumulators—sometimes a shilling was sent on a journey across a string of horses, earning five shillings on the first, thirty on the second, two hundred on the third, a thousand (or fifty pounds) on the fourth, and so on, if they all won, which they never did, except one morning when my dad came home from the night watch at the stable and woke everybody up to give us half a crown each, the only time he pulled off a big accumulator.

It was illegal to bet, except by post or telephone or at the actual races. People with telephones could bet even at the seaside or wherever they went for their holidays, but the people that did most of the betting did not have telephones. At home the women gave their money to a bookie's runner, the milkman, for example, who brought the winnings the next day. My dad didn't like anyone, especially my mum, to know or guess what he had won or lost, so his own runner was the nightwatchman at the stables.

Joe actually went to the races, at Kempton Park, or Sandown, or Hurst Park. He told stories if he came home in a good mood, for instance about the tipsters on the course, men selling tips on the day's races. Joe's favourite was a man known to us through him as "the old scruff." He was in his fifties, Joe thought, dressed, in all weathers, in a ragged raincoat held together with a safety pin, a shirt without a collar, worn-through mittens, and broken, see-through boots, laced up with string. He had glasses held on by elastic bands behind his ears, dislodged from time to time when he lifted his sleeve to wipe his nose on his cuff. I said he sounded like our rent collector and they all laughed but I meant it; he did. Joe said he had a BBC accent, so he must have come down in the world. Before he sold any tips, well before the first race, he used to give a talk on the afternoon's racing, and then before each race a mini-talk leading up to the selling of his tips, which he did by turning his back on the crowd and underlining his selection on your racecard. (Joe did a comical imitation of him.) Whenever Joe came home from the races, after we had found out if he'd won, the next question was "Did you see the old scruff?"

"Mind your language," my mum said automatically, reminding us we weren't old enough to be disrespectful of adults, whoever they were. But she was interested, too. She always had a bet on the Derby. Joe said the old scruff knew everything about the breeding of the runners, as well as their recent racing history and all the other factors that had to be taken into account. "The King," the old scruff would say, "bred this one himself, so it must be a threat, and it's dam was a stayer. But I think it lacks experience yet and I'm led to suspect that His Majesty is just giving him a run to find out his stamina, so I'll pass over that one and go on to the Duke of Tyrell who bought this one for his daughter when Mardi fell at Cheltenham and had to be put down. That was two years ago . . ." And so on.

Joe said he made it sound as if he knew the King personally. He charged tuppence a race, or a shilling to mark the whole program, and he was very good value, Joe said. Some of the other tipsters who sold their tips sealed up in envelopes sometimes sold different tips on the same race, thus making sure someone won, but Joe never caught the old scruff doing this. There were stories about his possible aristocratic background—"he was the son of an earl, cut orf without a shilling"— but my brother believed he was just a well-brought-up bloke who had lost everything he had at the races and it had caused him to lose touch except with the world of racing. (When I came across one of the versions of the story of the crippled blind old beggar who, at night, behind locked doors, removes his disguise to reveal a handsome, rich adventurer who has made a fortune from begging, I suggested to Joe that perhaps this was the case with the old scruff, but Joe said he didn't think so, not at tuppence a race.)

Big race days, like the Derby and the Grand National, brought out tipsters you never saw at any other time, Joe said, because there were more mugs about, like our sisters. The most famous tipster was Prince Honolulu, a black giant in brilliant-coloured robes and a turban, whose cry—"I gotta horse"—rang out over the Epsom Downs on Derby Day. Women felt that a very tall black man might be lucky, or have access to other kinds of knowledge, like voodoo, which gave him insights. But real punters, like Joe and my dad, consulted the old scruff.

On Saturday nights, the Band of Hope went round the pubs, collecting money so they could preach against the evils of drink and gambling. The people who drank two or three pints on a Saturday night were in no danger of being ruined by drink, and thus saw the Band of Hope as working in a good cause to save the real drunkards; they understood "gambling," too, to mean something foolish, wagering the money that should have been spent on food and clothes. "Having a bet," on the other hand, was one of the few harmless pleasures in life for a working man, for a bloke might have a bet every day at less cost to the household budget than the tropical fish his neighbour spent his money on. Of course, warning stories were handed down about the exceptions who slipped from "having a bet" to gambling, usually by frequenting dog tracks. The example held up to me by my dad when I started betting was of a man he knew who inherited three butcher shops and took to gambling. "He sold one shop," my dad said. "Done that in a week. Done the other two in a month. Then he done 'is 'ouse, then 'is car. At the finish, bloke at the stable saw 'im one night outside Wimbledon dog track—*no boots!*"

But for people like us, a piece of paper wrapped around a shilling slipped into the milkman's hand, and the result checked in the evening papers on the way home, might be the most interesting event of the day. The Band of Hope relied on people who had had a good day with the bookies to help pay for their campaign against gambling.

On Sundays after tea during the winter, they played cards, and we were allowed to watch for a while.

Joe invited a couple of mates, and sometimes two old neighbours from Kennington came, Mr. and Mrs. Earley, Uncle Fred and Aunt Em, non-relatives with honorary titles, and the only people we knew who owned a car, a large middle-aged saloon, in which they some-times took mum and any kids who were too young to be left to play on the street for a little outing to Hampton Court or Richmond. I liked the Earleys, we all did, and they liked us. They were the only adults I knew who never grudged other people their good luck. Everybody else seemed to be jealous of each other. ("Another one married, then, Daisy. I suppose you're pleased. The others don't come back to see you much, though, do they? What about the boys? Len still out of work?")

But Em said things like, "Did you hear that, Fred?" (Fred, my mum said, was as deaf as a beadle.) "Their Lily is engaged, too, now. I always knew she was waiting for the right one. Little dear. You let us know what she wants as a wedding present, Daisy. And while I think of it, Fred, give the kids their money."

Visitors, relatives and those we called relatives, like the Earleys, always gave the kids money. Aunt Rose gave my mum sixpence for all of us, and mum shared it out the next morning. Uncle Ted gave us a penny each. "'Ere you are, then. 'Ere's what you've been waiting for." Uncle Fred Earley gave us a threepenny bit each and tried not to let my mother see it so we could spend it all at once if we liked.

When there were outsiders at the card game, my brother dunned the men, including the guests, for the money for two or three quarts of beer, and later on my mother served cheese sandwiches and pickled onions. Everybody played—Chase the Ace, Lousy Lou, Newmarket— "simple games that the women can understand." If you were fourteen, you were earning money of some kind and responsible for your own weekly budget, so you were entitled to play. The first time Gladys played, at fourteen, she lost the lot—her dinner money, her season-ticket money—everything, and cried her eyes out. "Oh, bloody hell," my brother said. "Give her her money back," my mum commanded. "'Ere, all you winners: divvy up. Now, here's your money, miss, and now don't ask if you can play again. If you can't lose, you shouldn't be playing. I knew it would end in tears."

So if Gladys wanted to be allowed back in the game next time, she would have to show how much extra money she had over and above her weekly expenses that she could afford to lose, and give Mum the money she needed for the week to hold on to for her. But she never asked again.

Ron always said we worked so hard to be respectable there wasn't enough money left for food. Mum, he meant. After tea, Ron used to slope off to Joey Richards over on Western Road and cadge another tea from Mrs. Richards. There was always plenty to eat round at the Richardses', he said, even if they did use newspaper for tablecloths. Mum never knew about Mrs. Richards feeding him until afterwards, when he was in the merchant navy, or she would have put a stop to it. She was always on the lookout for people feeling sorry for us because there were so many kids. Once, a lady who I ran errands for gave me a big cake to take home. She said it was left over from a tea party she gave. When I gave it to my mum, she sniffed it, lifted it up, and showed me the bottom which was covered in green mould.

"Take it back and tell her we don't need her mouldy cakes. Go on, take it back. Now. Or I'll come with you."

So I did. Mum was wrong. Mrs. Jenkins didn't know about the mould because someone had brought the cake to her party. When I told Mum, she said, "Then your Mrs. Jenkins has got some sorting out to do, hasn't she?"

Ron was the runt of the litter. Even his teacher thought he didn't get enough to eat. He got the same as the rest of us, plus what Mrs. Richards fed him, but the school nurse said he had to have cod liver oil and malt and they sent home a big jar of it. Mum was mortified at first, seeing it as a reflection on the way she was bringing us up, then she marched up to the school and got enough cod liver oil and malt for all of us. There were no favourites in our house except Joe when he was still the only boy. Ron just burned his food up faster.

He had other problems: he was born with a squint and his eyesight was bad apart from that, his handwriting was poor, probably because he was left-handed, and he wasn't very good at arithmetic. None of this was his fault, but at that time, having trouble reading and writing was seen as a sign of dullness, and his handicap got him labelled a dunce, and no one thought much of his prospects. When he was fourteen and it was time for him to leave school, Dad got him a job in his yard, cleaning out the stables, which shows what they thought he was good for. "Young Bosher," they tried to call him until Ron wouldn't go to work and made my mum sign the papers for the merchant navy by threatening to run away anyway. Considering his qualifications and school record, he was lucky to get in, but they needed stewards as well as deckhands, and that's what he became, and finally he got enough to eat.

Ron knew he wasn't stupid, but being labelled like that separated him from the world, including us, and turned him into a loner, an original, someone who learned to think things out for himself. He had one very close friend, Joey Richards, the boy whose mother used to feed him if he was there at teatime, but he belonged to no gang. He sometimes took me with him on excursions into the neighbourhood, and tried to teach me the tricks of surviving on the street. Once he showed me what you have to do to get into a game of marbles if you only have one or two marbles. (Marbles, or alleys, we played along the gutter, aiming at each other's marbles using the junction of the kerbstone and the street as a bowling lane. You bowled in turn, trying to hit and win the marble of the boy you were playing with.) "Get a pocketful of stones," Ron said, "and jingle them when you ask someone to play. They'll play if they think you've got a lot to lose, otherwise they won't."

Another time he took me to Mitcham Fair, and showed me another side of his originality. The point of the fair, of course, was to go on the rides and to play the games, but we had no more than fourpence between us, all my mother was prepared to spare. As we walked around, I considered what to spend my tuppence on, which game of chance to invest in; Ron was fascinated by the money he saw passing into the gypsies' hands. Then as we passed the coconut shies, he proposed we pool our pennies and make an offer to the stall owner to buy a broken coconut. I went along with his idea, so we went home with some coconut to eat, but it wasn't much fun. I would rather have played one of the games. Ron said that it was stupid to risk losing your money like that, that the stall owners made sure it was hard to win, and we didn't have a chance. He worked out for himself that gambling was stupid, but he didn't stop me from wanting to have a go.

He liked having me for company if his only friend was not available, but he and Len, the nearest in age to each other, hardly ever played together. When any of us sought company, we found it outside the house rather than in a brother or sister close to us in age. In this way you could be yourself and not someone's little or big brother, and you could preserve your secret life from the people in the house. Len, in his turn, wanted nothing much to do with me, his young brother, and I refused to let my little sister into my world outside the house. So, being four years younger than he, I was no rival to Ron, just a little kid. But he made Len keep his distance. When Len was of an age to go to school for the first time, Ron had already been there for a year at least, but in infants' school, ages didn't matter much and a silly but well-meaning teacher thought it would be sweet to let the two brothers share a desk. When Ron saw Len coming, the story goes, he rushed to the door and slammed it in his face. "He's not coming in here," he screamed, again and again, until they found another room to put Len in. This room, Ron was saying, is mine, not ours.

Ron remained one of a kind: he couldn't stand pubs, he said, because listening to the people in them, which he understood was what they were all about, you heard the same tommyrot from the same people as you heard the night before. He preferred to read the paper, or, later, watch television. He might have become a hermit, but when he came out of the merchant navy he had put on weight and he had found a doctor to cure his squint, and discovered he had a talent for ballroom dancing, so he turned from a duckling into a swan, handsome in his uniform.

As Ron was solitary, Len was sociable. He liked pubs, but preferred his working man's club where he could sing, and he admired his mates and brought home stories of them from the earliest days, like our father. He got part of his identity from belonging to a gang, a group, a club of mates, full of wise ways and witty sayings. "You know what my mate, Charlie, at work says about the Labour party . . ."his stories would begin.

Ron told no such stories. In the eighties, when the whole family was drifting from its socialist roots towards Thatcherism, Ron watched, listened, saw through as much as he needed, and voted for whatever third party was running a candidate in Battersea, his riding.

At Christmas we all got enough to eat, even Ron thought so. Christmas Day always started out by being disappointing because Father Christmas did not have much left in his sack by the time he got to us. (The worst of it was having to hide our presents from our mates on the street who all did better at Christmas even if they didn't go to Sheerness in the summer.) The first time I was old enough to buy my mother a present, I shopped in Woolworth's for a small shiny statuette of a black girl with a dress made of tiny silk cords through which you could see and feel her bosom. I thought she was smashing. "Oh, Gawd," my mother said, giggling. "It's the thought that counts, I suppose," and hid it behind the framed photographs on top of the piano.

At Christmas, for the only time in the year, the kids still at school got eggs and bacon and fried bread and fried tomatoes for breakfast. We got through the rest of the morning with the marzipan cigars and chocolate fish that Father Christmas had left in our stockings, and then we all sat round the dining-room table for turkey with sage-and-onion stuffing, potatoes, parsnips, carrots, Brussels sprouts, and gravy. (Normally the young kids ate in the kitchen until they were old enough to go to work, calling through the door one by one at the end for permission to leave the table.) I thought the turkey course was overrated, the vegetables in particular, sodden and nasty. But then came the Christmas pudding with custard, and that was impossible to beat, and on top of the pudding, right after it, to show she didn't bear any grudges over the way we treated her Brussels sprouts, Mum served hot mince pies which by rights should have been saved until teatime. The King spoke to us on the wireless while we were eating the afters and the lights were on so it must have been past three o'clock. Then at seven or thereabouts, we all sat down for tea, the meal the kids had been waiting for.

In our house we pulled the crackers at teatime and put on paper hats, blowing snakes into each other's faces, and sounding noisemakers. Tea was cold meat, especially tongue, and chicken-and-ham pie, and tomatoes and lettuce and salad cream, and afterwards another mince pie if you wanted, and cake, Christmas cake with marzipan and icing, and jelly, and tinned fruit salad, and, best of all, trifle—sponge cake soaked in sherry and covered in custard. And some of us still had a chocolate Santa Claus left.

The men played cards at Christmas, too, nervier games for higher stakes, like Nap, and Brag, while the women cooked the turkey and gossiped in the kitchen. After a while the women got fed up with doing all the work and Joe would have to call a break for a couple of hours to show that the men were just playing cards to fill the time. The men generally managed to get in about four hours of cards on Christmas Day and the same on Boxing Day. They didn't play on Christmas night because the women demanded entertainment once Christmas tea was over and the washing-up done.

One of the first things my mum had scraped the money together for, even before we left the Buildings, was a piano. One of the strongest good memories she had was of a rare excursion to the theatre to see *The Merry Widow*, whose tunes she preferred to any others for the rest of her life, and the certain way to make her happy was to find someone who could play the tunes from the musical. The waltz tune, at least, was as central to growing up in our house as "God Save the King."

You couldn't, Mum said, expect people to enjoy themselves at a party without a sing-song. So at Christmas we sang. Vi had taught herself to play a bit, and she used to lead the sing-song while she lived at home. After she got married and moved into the country, Joe found a pal to take over on the piano. Once upon a time everybody had a party piece, though none of them had a voice, except, later, Len, who, though he had no natural talent, loved singing so much that he worked up a kind of street-singer's style, perhaps having inherited the genes of our grandfather, the singer of "Look into My Eyes and Tell Me That You Love Me."

All the adults had songs they were pressured to sing at Christmas. Aunt Rose warbled a little chorus of "Red Sails in the Sunset" while my mum kept her eye on us to make sure we didn't laugh; Mum sang "Just a Song at Twilight" on condition we all joined in after "Softly Come and Go." Dad sat swelling in the corner, waiting to sing his "Song of the Thrush," as my mother created a diversion to get us to pass over him. "He makes such a face," she said. "Closes one eye, puts his hand up to his ear like Paul Robeson did when we saw him on the halls, and then forgets the words. *And* he calls it 'The Song of the Frush,' as if we'd never left the Buildings. Tell him Vi can't remember the tune. Make him sing "Pack Up Your Troubles" instead, and we'll all join in."

That worked. We all sang "Pack Up Your Troubles," looking at Dad to show we were taking our lead from him. He nodded his head along with the song, finding a word where he could, usually at the end of a line. So his song became: "Nod, nod, nod-nod-nod-nod your old kitbag and nod, nod, nod. Nod, nod, a Lucifer to light your fag, nod, nod, nod, nod, nod," and so on. Then Joe shouted, "Well done, Pop," to show it was over, and just to make sure, would start a chorus of "Lily of Laguna" or—"Here's one for Mum"—"Daisy, Daisy, Give Me Your Answer Do," leaving my father not quite sure what had happened but pleased with himself and trying to remember the words to his other song, "I'm in Love with Two Sweethearts," which it was the fear of my mother's life he might actually try to sing, in front of her, on one knee. Actually, I don't think he got his style from Paul Robeson, but from the street-singers who used to come round on Sunday mornings, always one, sometimes more than one. They walked backwards down the street singing a ballad, hand up to the mouth (not ear), and people threw ha'pence to them from upstairs windows. My mum always threw them a ha'penny, just as she always gave something to match-sellers, especially if they were ex-soldiers and blind or missing an arm or a leg. "Always give a penny to a blind man," she taught us. She wasn't being kind; with her it was superstition, a way of warding off the fate that had not befallen her husband. She had lost a brother in the trenches.

I don't remember learning to read. I cannot remember a time when I couldn't read, but it must have begun somewhere. I remember my sister Vi buying me a book that was about two years too young for me, when I was seven or eight, which I hid until I could throw it away, but my earliest memories are of being able to read. At Christmas, I used to hide in the other room where the fire left over from teatime was still burning—Christmas was the only day of the year when there were fires in both downstairs rooms—to read my comics or the books I had taken out from the library. No one else minded—it was *my* Christmas, too, and they sort of pitied me as if it was not my fault if I would rather read than join in, like someone with a handicap. No one, that is, except one man, a family friend we were told to call "uncle," like Uncle Fred Earley. This "uncle," a cocky little man with small bright black eyes, made his living selling fruit from a barrow in the street markets. My parents had known him since their courting days. According to my mother, he was "as sharp as a tack." I never liked him because he used to make fun of my dad who wasn't as sharp as he was, treating him like a kind of stooge. When he went over the line into actually jeering, my mother stepped in to stop him, usually with a reference to some event in the past when, in her opinion, this uncle had been too sharp by half at the expense of others. (My mother and this man went back a long way, to the Draper Street market where she had met my father.) If he responded, there would be a row, but he usually shut up, fearing what my mother was holding in reserve. Most of the time my mother went along with the general opinion that this uncle was a caution, a card.

I didn't, and he knew it, so he kept an eye on me, and when he could, attacked the idea of me. "Not too sociable, is he, that one?" he commented, when I left the room in the middle of one of his stories. He liked an audience, and when I didn't join in, he found the fault in me, not in himself.

He thought he had his chance Christmas night. He had sung a solo, and then found me alone in the next room, reading. He went mad. "'Ere, Jack," he shouted, holding the door open. "Come 'ere. Look at this kid. 'Ere's the rest of us trying to 'ave a good time, Christmas night, and 'e's got 'is 'ead stuck in a bleedin' book. It's bloody unsociable, that's what it is, and you want to correct 'im. He does it deliberate."

My dad was never sure of himself socially away from the stables, especially around this uncle's sharpness, so he said, "Right. You. Len— Ron—Eric. Put that book down and come in and join the fam'ly at Christmastime."

Then behind him my mum appeared. "Let the boy stay where he is if he wants to. Come back in the other room. Doris is going to recite."

"Let 'im *stay*? Let'im *stay*! Let 'im sit 'ere, 'is bloody nose in a book, showing 'e's too good for us? You goin' to put up with that, Jack? Explain to 'er what's right."

Mum said, "Jack's got nothing to do with it. I'm 'ere, too. And as for insulting be'aviour, I remember a time when you shined in that regard."

And they were off, a blazing row fanned from the coals of all the old quarrels.

"I've 'ad enough of this," this uncle said soon. To his wife, "'Ere, missis, get your coat on. We're goin'."

But it was Christmas night and there were no more tube trains running so they had to stay over until the morning, and an hour later the singing had started up, and the conversational traffic was again flowing over the flimsy bridge put up mainly by my brother Joe, bustling around, starting up a quick game of McGinty's Dead, something like that, anything to get the talk into other channels.

And then, when everyone was getting organized for bed, some of them camping on piles of coats, my mother cornered me in the kitchen and closed the door. "Listen to me now, you," she said, quiet but serious. "You've gone too far, you 'ave. No more reading in company again. I'm not 'aving it. You live 'ere, you join in. Understand?"

Six

Lil's Wedding

APART FROM Christmas, weddings were the best feasts, the best times for getting lots to eat. When they asked you if you wanted seconds, they meant it.

The summer when Lil married Sid, they had the reception in the Boy Scout hut at the end of Colwood Gardens; it was called Atlasta Hall because it took them so long to build it. Sid came from Catford and he worked for John Lewis, the London draper, as a driver, like my dad, only motorized. Sid owned a car, an old saloon, and when he was visiting and staying late, at Christmas, say, he set out hurricane lamps in front and behind the car because he said otherwise you were supposed to leave your lights on. We thought the Fortescue Road gang would nick the lamps, but they were always there the next morning.

When Lil brought Sid home you could see she was very proud of him (and of having "clicked"), and he was just as proud of her. He called her Lily and asked us all to do the same, but Mum said he would have to put up with "Lil" because after twenty-odd years it was hard to change. She agreed that "Lil" did sound a bit common but we were in the habit now. Joe and May made the effort for Sid, and Dad tried but he couldn't always remember. The rest of us carried on with "Lil," swallowing the second *l* as always. The funny part was, Mum said, that Lily was what she wanted to call her in the first place. After Violet, Mum wanted to name all the girls after flowers, but the registrar told her that Lily was short for Lillian and that's what she would have to be registered as, and Mum had to do what he said.

Anyway, you always shortened names, otherwise people thought you were putting on airs. "Harold" was always "Harry" then, and "James" "Jim." Some names described a category; many oldest sons, like Joe, got called "Son" all their lives, and my mother's nickname was Daisy, which she shared with every fair-haired girl-child of her time. What I liked about Sid was that he made "Lily" sound, not formal or hoity-toity or soppy, but respectful, showing his respect for her. (He never expected anyone to call him Sidney, though, which was right because he was a "Sid" through and through.)

It was a white wedding, of course. Sometimes, on Saturdays, Sid earned extra money by driving for a car-hire firm for weddings and funerals, so he knew the proper form and he hired the right wedding clothes, striped trousers and a silk tie. Very posh, we thought he looked. My mum had been saving up her co-op dividends ever since Sid had proposed, and now she took us three boys up to Tooting Broadway to the co-op and bought us outfits of grey flannel blazers and shorts. She thought Dad's Saturday night-at-the-pub suit would do to stand up at the altar in, but Lil said he needed a new one so Mum said Lil would have to buy it, she didn't have any money for a new suit for him. So Lil bought him a nice grey suit from Burton's—the Fifty-Shilling Tailors—and Mum bought herself a nice two-piece costume, blue "heather-mixture," she described it as, to have something for best afterwards, to go to the seaside in.

Lil booked the church for two o'clock, the last legal time for a wedding according to an old law which was passed to keep the poor sober until they reached the altar, and we all walked down to the church which was just round the corner on Christchurch Road. Waiting in the church was the worst bit because the church was dark and smelled of coffin-wood; it was like a giant tomb itself, and we never went near the place normally so we didn't know how to behave. But once Lil and Dad had walked up the aisle and the vicar had done his job and asked us not to throw confetti on church property, Lily and Sid came down the aisle, and it was as if someone had punctured a balloon and let in some light, and we all grinned at Lily as she went by.

There was a hired car ordered for the happy couple to drive home in, and another one for the two mothers, and after the photograph was taken they drove round the corner and the rest of us walked home once we'd given them a bit of a start so they could have a minute to themselves. Everybody walking down Colwood Gardens in our best clothes.

The wedding breakfast, as they called it, though it was after three o'clock already, was catered by two local women. We were looking forward to it, knowing it would be the best kind of Sunday tea: ham, tongue, pork pie, sausage rolls, beetroot, cucumber, and lettuce, all arranged on plates before we went into the hall and sat down. Afterwards they brought round jelly, blancmange, tinned fruit, and cream, with Tizer for the kids and tea for the adults. Then came the speeches and everyone got a glass of champagne, with ginger beer for the kids but in champagne glasses, too, as the best man toasted the happy couple and Sid spoke, thanking Mum and Dad for giving him Lily, and Lil beamed at him for looking so handsome.

Afterwards they took the tables out and we all sat round the hall, his family on one side and ours on the other, the families inspecting one another and passing comment, then the best man announced the bar was open. There was a barrel of beer for the men and gin and port wine for the ladies and everyone had a drink while the little kids raced up and down the middle of the hall. Then the band arrived—an accordion, a trumpet, and a piano—and the dancing began. Sid and Lil started it off, of course, then Sid danced with Mum, which he said was the right thing (Sid was very keen on the right way of doing things. He told Mum once that she shouldn't serve Yorkshire pudding with roast pork, only with lamb or beef. "Silly bugger," Mum said, after he was gone. "You can serve batter pudding with anything you like.") Then everybody was dancing and having a good time and one of Sid's aunts fell down because the floor was too slippery, her husband said, but Mum reckoned she'd had too much gin. That passed off and Joe tried to collect together a few of the men to go back to the house afterwards for a hand of cards, but Mum put a stop to that. Not on Lil's wedding day, she said.

And then Lily and Sid, who had been missing for a while, came back, her in a nice two-piece and a little hat now, and we followed them outside on to the street to wave them off on their honeymoon. My dad kept walking round saying, "Right, That's three done. 'Oo's next while I've still got me new suit on?" and laughing his head off. Mum said to Joe, "Keep an eye on Dad. He's tipsy." I'd never seen Dad tipsy before.

Seven

The Boatman

AFTER INFANTS' school, everybody went to Fortescue Road Junior School until they were eleven, then they went to Singlegate Senior, except for the ones who got scholarships to the grammar school.

My first teacher at Fortescue Road when I was six was Mr. Young; I sat next to Mabel Tucker, who had brown curly hair. I woke up thinking about her in the morning and got to school early to make sure no one else sat next to her. Mr. Young used to smell of the paste we used to stick paper together with, and on Friday afternoon, if we had been good, he told us a story, an adventure story he made up.

After Mr. Young we had Miss Wait, but I still sat next to Mabel Tucker. Miss Wait had a cane like Charlie Chaplin's walking stick and one day she caned a boy named Arthur twice on each hand. Each time she hit him he shouted at her that he would bring his mum up to the school and she would bash Miss Wait, but she just waved for him to put his hand out again. Once, a boy wouldn't put out his hand to be caned, so Miss Wait fetched Mr. Jones, a knobbly old man who was the head teacher, and he took the boy away and when he came back he was crying.

When we were nine, Mr. Thomas took over the class and kept it until the scholarship exam which qualified you for grammar school. In the whole class of about thirty, ten of us were separated off by Mr. Thomas and trained for this exam. I didn't sit with Mabel now, though we were still pals, because her family didn't let her sit for the scholarship. Lots of the parents didn't want their kids to try for the scholarship. They said that too much education made kids grow away from their families, and they weren't having it. A lot of people thought that. One of them paid a special call on us to tell my mum that her son was just as clever as me but she didn't want a grammar-school snot-nose in the house, one who would end up looking down his nose at his own family. My sister said she was probably protecting the boy because she thought he might not pass the exam if he took it.

When this woman came, my mum didn't even know I was in Mr. Thomas's scholarship group. She had just made sure I went to school clean and fed, and left it up to the school to know what to do with me after that. When she found out about the scholarship group she wanted to take me out of it because she saw it as special treatment for me, and she didn't allow that in the family, but my sisters told her to let me try, so I stayed in it even after the war started.

First, though, I was evacuated to the country.

Up until now, the countryside was something that filled up the space between Colliers Wood and the seaside, a view of trees and fields and cows, like a picture framed by the train window, to be looked at on our way to the seaside. The country was a desert of grass, without buses or shops or even proper pubs. What pubs there were were humpy, my mum said, full of local yokels, all men, who talked funny and stared at you, nothing like London or seaside pubs, which were sociable places, a bit noisy and some of them a bit rough, but still, more lively after a hard day's work than the dead-and-alive holes in the country. They didn't even have lights in the country, and not even real streets in some places. The only time the country was all right was during hop-picking when you could take the whole family and live in a big tent, using your holidays to earn a bit of extra money.

Vi lived in the country now. Before we moved from the Buildings, she went on holiday to Cornwall and met a sailor, an officer in the reserve navy, and married him, and he got a licence to run a pub in the country and they ran it for three or four years until the war came along. "The George," it was called, Loddon Bridge, Nr. Reading, Berkshire, the address was. It was very old by Colliers Wood standards; my sister May said it was a George IV hunting box, a story which she had heard from the local vicar. It seemed to have been put together by hand, any old how, so that upstairs all the rooms were on different levels and the floor of the landing sloped every which way.

Vi's husband was one of the first to go to war, before it even started, and then Vi ran the inn herself, and in the summer of 1939 when it was obvious there was going to be a war she offered to take me for the duration as her personal evacuee. The thing was, she had two bedrooms to let which might have been commandeered by the billeting officer who had to house the evacuees that were coming down from London, so it was better to have me than some stranger. She put me in one bedroom and our sister May and her husband and baby in the other. May's husband worked for a timber merchant who travelled back and forth to his work in London by train. May used to wait outside by the river to wave at him as his train crossed the railway bridge on his way home.

The River Loddon runs into the Thames, and where it runs past The George it's wide enough and deep enough to drown in. I couldn't swim then, but I only fell in once and my brother-in-law got me out with a boathook. The George had a big vegetable garden at the back with an orchard with enough trees to nearly fill the pavilion, a big storage shed, with russet apples. On one side, between the pub and the river, Vi had a tea garden on a lawn, with iron umbrella tables painted white and those little iron fold-up chairs. In the summer, people could order tea and cakes to be brought out there in the afternoon, and drinks at night when the bar was open.

Three young ladies appeared one afternoon and asked me if they could have some lemonade. I ran to tell Vi, who lifted down a bottle of Schweppes lemonade, divided it into three glasses, and put them on a tray for me to take out. "What do we owe you, young man?" one of the young ladies said. She was joking—I was just a boy, but she was being nice, and I ran back and asked Vi who said I should charge fourpence a glass.

"But that's a shilling!" I said. "That bottle of lemonade only costs fourpence ha'penny!"

"It only cost *me* tuppence ha'penny, my lad, but those misses are getting waited on. You pay for service. Off you go."

I ran back. "Fourpence each. A shilling." I held my breath.

"There you are, then." She handed me the shilling, smiling.

When they had gone I collected up the glasses and found two pennies under hers. I ran after her but they were already in their car. I told Vi.

"That's a tip," she said. "For you. See? There's money in this game."

I saw. But I soon saw that there was more money in the boats.

The river ran for miles in both directions. Robbie and I used to go over to Tooting Bec park sometimes on Sundays and hire a rowboat on the pond there, so I knew how to row. Vi had a little rowboat I used to take out to see how far I could go but I always got tired before I got to a weir or anything like that. Vi had a lot of boats that she used to hire out, punts, with cushions, and some skiffs for those who fancied themselves as rowers. The punts had to be paddled because the bottom of the river had too many holes for poling, and mostly it was young couples who hired them for courting. They used to paddle out of sight

71

of the inn and tie the boat to a branch of a tree and spend all the afternoon kissing each other.

I was the boatman. Vi had a gardener, Mr. Foster, a fierce little ginger-haired man in Wellington boots who kept telling me to leave the apples alone when he saw me in the orchard. Vi told me to be polite to him because soon gardeners would be hard to find. When Vi's husband went off to sea, Mr. Foster helped out with the boat-hiring at first, but he told Vi that was not his trade and she should find someone else. When I came, she got me to do it.

I thought it was smashing. We charged a shilling and sixpence the first hour and a shilling an hour after that, and sometimes they would owe three and sixpence or even four and sixpence on a sunny afternoon. I used to write up the time they went out with a piece of chalk on the slateboard inside the boathouse, and the time they came back. They often gave me tips. The change from two florins for three hours was sixpence, and I learned to be slow handing it to them to give them time to tell me to keep it. Sometimes, if they had had a nice afternoon kissing, I would get more.

Sixpence bought a lot, all the sweets I could eat, but I had to be careful. Vi sold chocolate and potato crisps in the pub and I didn't want to be seen eating anything that she sold and might have thought I had nicked from the pub. Ice cream was safe, as was licorice, sherbet, and the loose sweets sold from large glass jars. Any chocolate I bought I ate on the way home from the sweetshop, in Earley. Probably Vi would have believed me that I had bought the sweets from my tips, but she might have told my mum who would have been more suspicious, so I didn't say anything. Vi also gave me pocket money for looking after the boats and that and the tips was what she thought I was spending.

So I was as happy as a prince, having this important job, making tons of money, and spending it on sweets and comics which I could buy in Earley. I used to walk to Earley in the mornings when there weren't many customers. If someone wanted a boat when I wasn't there, Mr. Foster would look after them. Sometimes I went for a row in the small rowboat, which we never let out because I might have to row after a punt that got loose, or look for one that should have come back. Sometimes people got out of their punt farther along the river and walked away so as not to have to pay.

Vi and May were smashing cooks compared to my mum. I had an egg for breakfast every morning, always butter on the bread, never margarine, and two courses for dinner which May called lunch, with ham or pork pie for tea. Vi and May also set about teaching me the manners they had taught themselves since leaving the Buildings, like cutting the top off my boiled egg instead of tapping it and picking the shell off in bits; and breaking off a bit of bread with my fingers instead of taking a bite out of the slice. Dry bread, that is, the kind you got with soup. It was all right to hold a slice of bread and butter in your hand.

I had my own bedroom with a big sweet-smelling bed, and at night I could hear customers in the pub downstairs, and Vi's shout at closing time—"Come on you blokes," she shouted two or three times—and the traffic on the road past the inn, and the lights of the cars went across the ceiling in patterns that followed each other. Vi bought me pyjamas, which I'd never had before, none of us had. In Kennington and Colliers Wood we slept in our shirts.

Although Vi was my sister, she was gone from the Buildings before I knew her so she was a bit of a stranger, and I was on my best behaviour all the time. One night the door to my room jammed because it was so old and warped out of shape, and I wanted to pee but couldn't get out, so I peed in the copper kettle in the fireplace. The next day I tried to wait until the coast was clear to empty it, but there was always someone about so I left it. I could have told my mum about it, and if it had been Gladys or Doris I was staying with, I could have told her, but I was too shy to tell Vi because I didn't know her very well, so I left it there.

The other thing about it was that it got a little bit lonely having no mates around, especially Robbie. After a while, Vi realized this and she got one of the people who worked for her to send his son over to play with me, and that was all right. I liked him, although he was a bit of a yokel, I thought, and he didn't even have as good manners as I had in Colliers Wood, before May taught me. He ate with his mouth open, with his knife and fork in the air, and didn't ask to be excused before he got down from the table, and he always said yes if he was offered more and wanted some. (My mum had taught us all to say "No, thank you," to be polite.)

Still, we played a lot of good games together, in the orchard and along the river bank, and we tried to sink one of the punts, jumping up and down on one end, until Mr. Foster stopped us. But I was still on my own a lot.

The only time the war came near was one afternoon when I was in the apple-scented pavilion, lying in a hollow on a great pile of russet apples, where I thought no one could see what I was doing, and a German bomber came over and dropped a stick of bombs, four, I think, that went crump, CRUMP, CRUMP, crump as they straddled the inn and me. I thought God had been watching and sent the bomber to punish me.

Eight

Crime and Punishment

IN THE meantime the boats were very busy and sometimes I collected a lot of money. Did I ever think of stealing some of it? Did I ever *not* think of stealing any? I was from Colliers Wood by way of Kennington, and nicking stuff was as natural as breathing, so long as it was absolutely safe. It wasn't morality that kept us honest. You didn't steal because your family—my mother—had done a good job of letting you know the penalties: from being skinned alive by her, then handed over to your father when he came home to finish the job, then off to Borstal where you would be fed bread and water and knocked about continually by the jailers, and finally kicked out of the house— "I'm not having thieves in this house!"

That was why I didn't try to swindle my mother when I was sent to buy an egg. Rendell's, the shop around the corner from Colwood Gardens, sold four kinds of eggs: penny-farthing eggs, penny-ha'penny ones, penny-three-farthing ones, and tuppenny ones. They went up in size but the penny-farthing eggs were the same size as the penny-ha'penny ones. The difference was that the penny-ha'penny ones were guaranteed. If it was bad when you got it home, Rendell's would change it. But with a penny-farthing egg you took a chance.

They were usually all right, but you took a chance. The thing was you could buy a golly bar, a stick of toffee the size of your finger, for a farthing, so if you were sent to buy a penny-ha'penny egg, you could buy a penny-farthing egg and a golly bar and hope the egg was good. If it wasn't, then you were caught because you couldn't take it back and change it. Although I got very close, I never got up the nerve to buy a penny-farthing egg.

The closest I got to stealing outside the house—apart from shoplifting chocolate bars with Robbie—was one afternoon after Sunday school. Sunday school was held in a community hall on the other side of the rec. We all had to go until we were about seven or eight; my mother treated it as a kind of inoculation, a "just-in-case" measure. "You never know," she used to say. Normally, no one in my family, or any other I knew of, ever went near a church, although all of us felt that the church was the only proper place to get married in, to die from, and, for some, to get christened in. ("I never had the last three christened: that new vicar got up my nose—kept coming round, collecting for this and that and wanting to see us in church. The old vicar left you alone. He was a nice old boy.") We were sent off to Sunday school to find out what it was all about (but never to speak of it inside the house, like sex).

There were two kids in Sunday school, Ernie and Ray, brothers, thieves, sort of mates of Robbie's from one of his other worlds. They were a bit common: once, in their house, I heard them all—mother, Ernie, Ray, and two sisters—sing a rollicking version of "Mademoiselle from Armentières," which opened with the line, "A fart went rolling down the hill, parley-vous . . ." I felt very embarrassed, as if the mother had come downstairs in her knickers in front of us.

Ernie and Ray had noticed that the ha'pennies we took to Sunday school went into a little wooden box which was left in a small back room. Ernie, the elder brother, had also seen that the window of the toilet was always left open, and had found out that once you were in the toilet you could break into the small back room with no trouble. After Sunday school was over and the teachers had gone home the three of us ducked back through the bushes and made sure that we were out of sight of anyone walking down the path to the rec.

To get in the window, Ray, the younger brother, would have to stand on Ernie's shoulders; I was the lookout. "We'll share the money out equal," Ernie said. Then Robbie came along the path that led from the rec and was invited to join in. He listened to what we were planning, then flicked his head at me, ordering me to go along with him, saying to the others, "His dad sent me to find 'im."

"My dad's *asleep*," I protested, once we were away from the brothers. "He's always asleep on Sunday afternoons. Besides . . ."

Robbie interrupted. "If you get caught, they'd say you was the one who did it. I know them. Don't listen to them."

And the next day we heard that they did get caught. Someone saw them breaking in and the police arrived and they were had up before the magistrates.

But I was still inclined towards stealing, most of us were if it could be done in safety, and the boat money was irresistible. Even if I was caught, my sister wouldn't send me to Borstal. So, from the time I saw the opportunity, I never considered not stealing some of it. And besides, I'd found a need for the money. The tips were all right for sweets, but I had started a stamp collection, and I took the bus into Wokingham as often as I could to buy stamps. The ones I wanted cost more than I could get from tips.

And so I took the next step. Five boats had been hired by a party of "young hounds" (Vi's word) and each other's sisters. Vi had gone to London, leaving the pub in charge of the woman who helped out on Saturdays. I chalked up the time the five boats moved off, and when they came back, collected the money, walked twice round the garden to make sure Mr. Foster hadn't looked in on his day off, wiped out the record of the fifth boat, and put a mere fourteen shillings in the cigarette tin where we kept the day's take, pocketing the three and sixpence, to be hidden later in the actual, real, hollow tree I had discovered on the other bank of the river.

And so it started. The swag grew until there were two or three pounds in a little leather bag I once kept my marbles in, tucked away in the old hollow tree, more money than I had ever handled. Now I had to spend it. Apart from stamps, I wanted a big Meccano set. Vi had bought me a starter set, with enough wheels and tiny girders to make a model hand-cart, but the set came with a leaflet picturing what could be done with a giant set: gantries, windmills, trucks—the possibilities were unlimited. But it was out of the question; I could never have accounted for it. So I had to be satisfied with buying stamps. I already had a little collection, bought in Colliers Wood with halfpence, mostly German inflationary issues, printed in the millions. I knew what I really wanted, not penny blacks or cape triangulars, but those gorgeous ones of the British colonies, the King's head in one corner of a beautiful picture of a giraffe (Kenya, Uganda, and Tanganyika), and all the other works of art from Africa, the Caribbean, and the South Seas.

Then, in Wokingham, I found a dealer and began to spend my money. One by one I brought them home and fixed them carefully in my stamp album. There was no need to show them to anyone yet; I could do that later, at home, when I saw Robbie again. For the time being I could enjoy gloating over the little Stanley Gibbons album I kept in the cardboard suitcase under my bed along with the two lead soldiers, the propelling pencil I found in one of the boats, and the army badges.

And then, one day, the stamp dealer asked me my name, and I thought I'd been caught. "William Brown," I said.

"Where's all the money coming from then, William?" The stamp dealer with a look invited his hovering wife to listen.

"My paper round."

"You're not from around here. You're a Londoner. You don't have a paper round."

I looked out the window, thinking. "That's my Dad," I said and ran.

For three days I lived in fear, but the dealer never appeared at the inn. Nobody set any traps, like they did in the stories I was reading, and no one asked me why I rowed over to the old hollow tree every day. No, this was how it happened.

After a few days the habit of stealing some of the boat money came back, but I didn't take as much as I did before because now that I couldn't buy stamps I didn't know what to do with the money. Then, one day, the fair came to a field in Earley and my sister gave me a shilling to visit it. It had been a quiet day on the river and all I had in my pocket was a sixpenny tip. Of course, it occurred to me what a good time I could have at the fair with the hoard from the old hollow tree, but Mr. Foster was looking after the boats for the afternoon, and with him watching I couldn't think of an excuse to row across the river before I went to the fair.

Even so, one and six was a lot of money and I was surprised how quickly it disappeared. Two rides, a go on the shooting gallery, and a coconut shy, and I only had three pennies left. I stopped by a stall in a round tent where you could roll pennies down a wooden slot in the hope of landing on a winning square. On the second try my penny rolled into a sixpenny square. The gypsy lady in charge dealt me six pennies and moved on. The booth was large and busy, and the gypsy had to circle around the inside, picking up the losing pennies and paying out the winners. I rolled down another penny and won six more; I did it again, and again, and again, until I was out of breath with excitement. There was a tiny warp in the surface of the table just beyond my wooden chute, and if my penny reached this warp, travelling at the right speed, it fell over into the square. I won about eight times, and then, deliberately, under her eye, put the penny too high in the chute and lost. I left the booth for a while and threw some more balls at the coconuts, but nothing compared with winning pennies.

When I went back, another gypsy had taken over and I won another four shillings before she started to watch me and I had to deliberately lose again. Now I developed a system, winning a couple of times, going for a walk, coming back to win again as soon as my chute was free. Soon, both my pockets were crammed with big copper pennies, and the attendant in charge of the tent with the slot machines changed some of them for me into silver, and most of the rest I spent on rides, shooting ranges, and the other games, until I'd had enough, and I walked home with a story to tell.

I arrived back at The George, passing through the saloon bar to get to the living room behind. The barman was behind the counter, talking to a customer. His face was serious. "Your sister wants to see you," he said. "In the back room."

The customer turned round and I nearly swooned when I saw the face of the stamp dealer from Wokingham. I thought it was the end for me. But the man just said, with a sly look, "Who's this, then?"

"Her brother. Staying with her for the duration."

"Has he got a name?"

"Eric."

"Lucky boy, living in a pub." The dealer took a swig. "Interested in stamps, son?"

"Not much."

"I thought you collected them," the barman said, holding up the flap of the counter to let me through.

"Used to. Don't now."

The dealer smiled, picked up his change, winked at me. "Cheerio," he said, and left.

"She's waiting."

I ran through, dizzy with relief at the dealer's strange loyalty, and slipped into the living room where my sister was waiting with the woman who helped out on Saturdays.

"Come here," my sister said. "Turn out your pockets." She said it sort of sadly, kindly.

Now it looked as if the dealer had told on me after all, as was natural. The scene in the bar had been a tease, a cat-and-mouse scene, while all the time the dealer knew what waited for me in the kitchen.

My sister pointed to the kitchen table to show me where to put the money from my pockets.

"Don't have to," I mumbled.

"You want me to tell Mum?"

Threat enough. I emptied both pockets; I still had a dozen pennies, and several of the shillings that I had changed back. It was a pile the size of a fist. My sister looked at the money without saying anything. The face of the woman who helped out on Saturdays was shining.

"Where'd you get it?" my sister said at last.

"Won it."

Headshakes.

"I'll ask you again. Where'd you get it?"

"Won it."

Now she'd used up the threat of telling mum; it wouldn't have been fair to use it twice. She tried to shame me. "Don't tell lies," she said. "Don't *lie*," she said like a schoolteacher.

This wasn't fair. *Everybody* from Kennington lied to the authorities. She knew that. She'd lived there once. She had no right to be on the other side.

"I'm not lying. I won it."

The woman who helped out on Saturdays said, "They don't let you win. Only once or twice p'raps. Our Fred lost six bob on that roll-the-penny game." She gleamed at my sister, encouraging her to carry on.

"You took it out of the boat money, didn't you?"

"No. I won it."

And then I saw what she needed. A little brother who stole was one thing, a thief *and* a liar shown up in front of the woman who helped out on Saturdays was something else. I could feel her wanting me to tell the truth.

"Some of it was tips," I said.

"Not that much." She looked at the pile on the table. "Elsie, here, watched you all night. You went on all the rides."

"Spent a fortune," the woman said.

So it had been *this* rotten cow. The dealer had kept quiet, after all.

"Some of it probably *was* tips," my sister offered. "Not all of it, though, was it?"

"Not all of it, no."

"Some of it was boat money, wasn't it?"

I nodded, a quarter of an inch.

"Make 'im say," the woman who helped out on Saturdays said. "Go on."

"That's all right, Elsie," Vi said. "Leave us alone now."

"Make 'im say," the woman repeated as she went through the door.

"Don't tell Mum," I said, when we were by ourselves.

She shook her head. "What are we going to do with you, then?" I could feel her yearning across the space between us. We'd never touched each other; you didn't hug in our family. "Will you promise never to take the boat money again?"

"Oh, yeah." Then, suddenly, "I don't want to look after the boats any more."

"You can still look after the boats . . ."

"I don't want to."

"What do you want to do, then? Help Mr. Foster?"

And then it came. "I want to go home," I said, and as I said it I did, want to go home, back to bread and margarine, back to the other liars and thieves on Colwood Gardens, back to a world of crime and punishment I understood, back to Robbie's world. "I want to go home," I said again. "Let me go home."

"P'raps that's best. Don't say I sent you, mind. If I take you up to London and put you on the right tube, can you manage?"

"'Course I can." We used to ride all day on the tube for a penny, changing trains. She was treating me like a kid. "You don't have to come up to London, even. I can go on the train myself." Then, to be certain, I said again, "Don't tell Mum."

"No, she'd kill you. What'll we say? You got homesick?"

"That'll do. In the morning, then?"

She sniffed and looked down at her hands.

"It's not *your* fault," I said. "I'll just say I got homesick."

She nodded and sniffed again. "I thought p'raps you might want to stay on here, even when the war's over. We would have sent you to Reading Grammar School," she said.

It was tempting because I was right in the middle of my schoolboy-story period, the *Hotspur* stories especially, stories which all took place in schools like Reading Grammar. But Colwood Gardens won. The thing was, I wasn't at home at The George. My sister was nice to me but we weren't friends—there was twenty years between us—and she wasn't trying to be a mother. She was just an old sister I didn't know very well, and though I knew she was trying to get me to better myself, like her, I found it a strain.

She did my washing and ironed it herself, and drove me to Earley station the next afternoon, and I caught the train to Waterloo.

I didn't row across the river first and get the money out of the old hollow tree. If I'd been caught doing that, I think Vi *would* have told my mum. She thought I'd just nicked the odd sixpence or shilling, but the leather bag was nearly full. As far as I know, it's still there, like the pee in the copper kettle.

Nine

Mr. Thomas

IT WAS smashing being back in Colliers Wood. The war hadn't properly got going yet, although Joe had been called up because he was in the Territorial Army, so I still went to Fortescue Road Junior School, and played out on the street with the same gang. Robbie was a year older than me and he was gone now, to Singlegate Senior School until he was fourteen, and he had some new mates from Singlegate, though we were still mates on Saturdays and Sundays because he still lived just round the corner on Clarendon Road.

It was smashing being back at school, too, because I worshipped Mr. Thomas. Everybody did. When he came out of Colliers Wood tube station in the mornings there was a gang of kids waiting to run alongside him as he walked to school through the rec, asking him questions like, "What were you like when you were our age, Mr. Thomas?" and "Where do you go on your 'olidays, Mr. Thomas?" and "Do you have any brothers or sisters, Mr. Thomas? What are their names?"

Anything to be noticed.

Mr. Thomas didn't just teach us our lessons; he tried to teach us everything he thought we needed. He told us all to buy toothbrushes and he used to look at our teeth every morning to make sure we had cleaned them. A few of the kids already had toothbrushes—I didn't—but if any of the others said they didn't have the money, he bought them one himself. This got him into trouble with some of the parents when the kids took their toothbrushes home, because they didn't like the idea that some schoolteacher was pointing out a deficiency in their upbringing, and besides, in one or two cases, they didn't agree with teeth-brushing.

We bought little pink cakes of Gibbs dentifrice for a ha'penny each, and some of these Mr. Thomas paid for, too. Once he used me as an example of what would happen if we didn't use our toothbrushes.

Every year a woman we called Nitty Nora came round looking for fleas and lice on our heads, and also sometimes a dentist from the council looked at our teeth. One day when the dentist came to me he said I had to have all my back teeth out. My mum took me up to St. Thomas's, which was near Kennington, a long way from Colliers Wood, but it was always our hospital. My mum didn't trust the local hospital; St. Thomas's had looked after Ron's double pneumonia, May's diphtheria, Gladys's scarlet fever, and sewed Len's finger back on when he had chopped it off in the coal cellar. And the time May poured the boiling cabbage water over my arm when Mum was ill in bed, and my arm turned into a big blister all the way from my shoulder down to my elbow, Mum made her take me up to St. Thomas's, never mind the dinner still cooking. You couldn't beat St. Thomas's.

The night after they took my teeth out I woke up with a mouth full of lumps of clotted blood, and my pillow was soaked with it. My mum gave me a piece of clean cloth to hold over my mouth and we walked to Robinson Road, where the all-night trams turned round, about a mile away, and caught the tram to St. Thomas's, an hour's journey away. There the night doctor, with a nurse alongside, lifted out the bloodclots, pulling them free from my gums, and told me to spit it all out. But there was nowhere to spit. I looked at my mother, because she was the one in charge of where I could spit, and she looked at the nurse, who nodded, and my mum whispered, "It's all right," and I spat it all out on the clean, disinfected marble floor. The doctor pulled all the rest of the loose bits away from my gums and made me spit them out, too, and the nurse called a skivvy over to clean up the floor.

We took the tram back only as far as Stockwell, because I kept falling asleep and choking, and my mum left me to stay the night with Aunt Rose, who lived in Stockwell, while she went home to see to the rest of the family. When I woke up the next day, Aunt Rose made me a bowl of warm bread and milk, but it was so much like the stuff I had left on the hospital floor—not the taste, but everything else about it— that I couldn't get it down, so she gave me a cup of tea and a digestive biscuit, and I managed that all right. Then she wrapped my face up in a clean piece of cloth and tied a scarf round my head to keep it in place and put me on the tram home.

Mr. Thomas told us that plimsolls, or gym shoes, were bad for our feet, and we should ask our parents for shoes or boots. (I always wore shoes because my mum thought boots were common, and only very poor kids wore plimsolls.) Some of the kids stayed away from school when their boots were being mended. That was always an acceptable excuse for Mr. Thomas.

He asked us not to fart in his classroom—"blowing off," he called it—and to bring a piece of rag to school to use as a handkerchief. All winter he taught us everything he thought we should know—arithmetic, spelling, drawing, the names of the continents and the seas—all that—and that was the best year I ever had in school. He made the ten scholarship pupils sit in a special section of the class and gave us extra spelling tests and extra arithmetic, and general-knowledge tests. He gave us little cards to take home at night with ten questions on them, and we had to write out the answers neatly in whole sentences in our exercise books for the next day. That was my first homework.

The war was very quiet at first. Some of the kids who had been evacuated when war broke out came back a few weeks later, and everything carried on as normal, except for the rationing, which we didn't notice much at first. Joe came home on embarkation leave with a pal from Croydon, before they went to France "to hang out their washing on the Seigfried line." He was one of the first soldiers on our street, and we were all proud of him. Then, just as the scholarship exam was getting near, Hitler seemed to be winning the war and there was talk of being invaded and the school closed because a lot of the kids were being sent away again. The fire brigade used the playground to practise rolling dustbins across it with their hoses.

Because of Mr. Thomas, what was left of the scholarship group still got lessons in the houses of the some of the pupils, mostly in Kenny Field's house where his mum gave us milk and cake after the lesson. My mum said she was too busy to do anything like that but I think she was just nervous of strangers inspecting the inside of her house, especially Mr. Thomas.

In the spring of 1940, when the time came, we took the 152 bus to Mitcham County School at Fair Green to write the scholarship examinations, in English, general knowledge, and arithmetic, I think. They told us to bring a pen, a pencil (my sisters had bought me a Platignum pen-and-pencil set), a ruler, and a bottle of ink. That was my first examination and because of Mr. Thomas's teaching I thought it had been specially composed for me.

Four or five of Mr. Thomas's stars won scholarships, including me. When the letter came, my sisters got excited because my mum still wasn't sure if she wanted me to go even now I had won it. ("There'll be no money coming in from him until he's sixteen," my "uncle" said, when he heard. "It'll be all pay out with that one.") My sisters insisted, but my mum was afraid now that she might not have done a good job in teaching me the proper manners for a grammar school. She was nervous for herself and her house, too, about keeping her end up if I brought any "college" boys home. My sisters argued with her, and in the end my mum walked me to the corner of the street to post the letter. Just before we dropped it in the letter box, she made one last try to make sure I knew what I was taking on. "Now you be sure," she warned. "Sure you want to go. You can't drop out if you don't like it. You have to go for five years. You can't chop and change about." Back to the other stream, she meant, to Singlegate, and leave school at fourteen.

But I was too full of Billy Bunter stories not to want to go. I wanted a school uniform and a cap and to buy stuff at a tuck shop. And because of Mr. Thomas, I wanted to stay in school for the rest of my life. "I want to go," I said.

"You sure?"

"Yeah."

"No going back, mind."

"I know."

"Put it in the box yourself, then."

And I did.

Then I got my last lesson from Mr. Thomas, the first one in this new world. On a warm evening in the early summer I was playing football in the street with the kids I would soon leave behind, when Mr. Thomas appeared on a bicycle and called me over. Seeing Mr. Thomas out of school was so strange that the other boys stopped playing to watch and listen.

"Have you heard the results of the scholarship exam, yet?" he asked.

"Yeah."

"Did you pass?"

"Yeah."

"When did you hear?"

"Last week."

"You didn't come and tell me, did you?"

No one had taught me to. I couldn't say that to him but I had no other answer. I knew right away, though, that I should have. "I forgot," I said.

"All the others came to see me, to tell me they had passed. Anyway"—he put out his hand for me to shake—"well done. But I wish you'd come and told me yourself."

He didn't smile, but I understood that he wasn't telling me off. I'd just let him down by not going to the school to tell him, because it was *his* exam that I had passed.

He cycled away, and I never saw him again.

"Who was that?" my mother called from our front gate.

"Mr. Thomas, our teacher."

"What did he want?"

"He wanted to know if I'd passed."

"Didn't he know?"

"Course he did."

"Then what did he really want? Did you say thank you?"

"Course I did," I lied, shouting, nearly screaming at her, knowing immediately that I could not face all the "Why didn't you's?" from her, all the instructions to "Run after him and do it now," or "You'll have to go to school in the morning and tell him." She'd even make sure what words I would say as if I didn't know.

I turned back to the game. It wasn't my fault, I told myself. Nobody had told me that's what you're supposed to do. But that didn't stop me from feeling rotten. I looked for someone to punch but in the end just pushed a kid away from the ball, hoping he would push back and we could have a fight.

From now on I was on my own. My family had no idea what went on at a "grammar" school. (It was a county school, really, not a proper grammar school.) My mother had taught me everything she knew about manners, mostly to keep my mouth closed when I ate, and to refuse second helpings of anything. She had tried to get me to sign off my rare letters—"And oblige"—but even at eleven I knew she was the only one still saying that; Mr. Thomas had taught us to write "Yours faithfully." (My father wanted me to sign off, "Your humble and obedient servant," which he insisted was the proper way to end any letter.)

Then there was Dunkirk. Joe came home from the evacuation of Le Havre, and he sat in the corner, looking, my mother said, "like a tiger." She meant "like a cornered animal," I think, but she read almost nothing and had very few clichés to hand. Joe was one of the last off the beach. Because of varicose veins, he never got into the infantry proper, but was recruited into the service corps, looking after the equipment and supplying the kitchens with stores. He never realized until then how hard Dad worked, he said, lifting frozen sides of beef all day. But when the Germans rolled over the Maginot line and the French packed it in, the main thought of the English generals was to get as much of the army back across the Channel as they could, for the invasion they felt sure was coming. So they evacuated the fighting troops and left the odds and sods, like Joe and his mates, as a rearguard, to slow up the tanks. Eventually Joe and his mates were the only ones left and they got permission to leave themselves. Joe couldn't swim but he waded out to a small boat with his pal from Croydon who could, and then when they got to the boat his pal went under and never came up. When he came on leave, Joe had to go and visit his pal's parents to tell them how it had happened.

A neighbour over the garden fence said, "We might lose this one, ever thought of that?" My father said, "No, and we're not bleeding well going to, either, so sling your fucking hook out of here with that kind of talk and don't come back."

I'd never heard him swear like that before.

Six of them were gone now, and finally the rest of us each had our own bed.

All that summer we looked up to the sky and watched the Battle of Britain. And then came the blitz. But first there was the Mitcham County School for Boys.

My mother applied to the local council for a grant for my uniform, and they gave us two guineas, and we went up to the official school shop in Mitcham and bought the shorts, the socks, the shirts, the tie, the blazer, and the cap, all in the school colours, and the shorts and singlets for gym. While we were in the shop, she also bought me some underpants "like the other boys will be wearing," in case the ones I had were the wrong kind. Once, two or three years before, I had gone to a Boy Scout camp in Ashtead Forest and I saw that all the boys except me had underwear on. When I came home I asked my mum if she would buy me some underwear like the other kids, and right away she put on her hat and coat and took me on the tram up to the co-op in Tooting Broadway, where she bought me some underpants. She didn't say much, but she was in a funny state, I could tell. Later on she told my dad she was "mortified"—one of her favourite expressions— but I don't know what she was mortified about.

My sisters bought me a satchel, and on a morning in September I caught the 152 bus to Fair Green, along with half a dozen other boys of different sizes.

On our first day a boy went home at dinnertime and it took a week to coax him back. There were no Mr. Thomases here that I could see, and none appeared in my time. Everyone seemed to be waiting for me to do something wrong; masters wore gowns and looked like jailers; the older boys, from the sixth-form prefects all the way down to the twelve-year-olds in the next form above us, tried to look superior in front of the new boys. I wondered where these older boys came from. There were no young gents like that in Colwood Gardens. Then, in the playground, as we were waiting to be called in, a boy standing next to me shouted, "'Ere, Jonesy," to a passing youth in long trousers who looked irritated at being called out to. The boy turned to me. "He lives on our street. His name's Bernard, but he asked me not to call him that here. What's your name?"

"Eric."

He shook his head. "Your proper name."

"Wright."

"That's it. Say that. Wrightie. Mine's Munnings. My father's a printer. What's yours?"

"He's a furniture mover. He's got his own van. He can carry a piano downstairs on his back." Everyone admired the story of my grandfather, so I gave it to my father.

"All by himself? Cor! Let's sit together."

And so we did for the few days until the place was familiar. Munnings saw right away how things worked, or he was told how by Jonesy. At any rate, he made it a lot easier than it would have been without him. After a week, Munnings and I parted because by now I had found a couple of mates and in those days he was essentially a cheerful loner, but we stayed on good terms.

Right away I stumbled badly in most of the subjects except English, and I never properly recovered. I missed Mr. Thomas very much. For one thing, he knew that everything was up to him, that it was a rare boy at Fortescue who had a parent who could help his upwardly striving ten-year-old son with his schoolwork. But at

Mitcham they gave us homework which I had to do at the dining-room table with five or six other people in the room, listening to the wireless. Mum wouldn't allow any other lights in the house, even if the other rooms were warm enough. I could have done it for Mr. Thomas, but the thing was these new teachers didn't teach us—they taught *at* us, so you could look at them and think about something else, which you couldn't with Mr. Thomas. The French teacher was French, and I couldn't understand a word he was saying. The only one I took to was Mr. Stevens who taught math, and made sure you were listening. Because of him, I was good at math, though I wasn't naturally clever at it. The worst news was "PT."

PT was taught by an instructor who liked to put boys through their paces, as he called it. My clearest memory of PT is of him slashing repeatedly with a swagger stick (he was some kind of ex-serviceman) at the legs of a boy on a high beam. The boy was terrified of heights and terrified of the teacher and he shook so hard as he straddled the beam ten or twelve feet up in the air that the whole structure rattled, and still the teacher slashed away, shouting, "Come on, boy, get moving." He only stopped when Mr. Perry, the caretaker, looked in the door to see what the noise was all about. The same teacher liked to set up boxing matches among the older boys, and if they didn't mix it up properly, he put on the gloves himself and showed them how to knock each other about.

One big benefit of PT was the showers, the first constant hot water I had known, water that cleaned you off and warmed you up after a freezing two hours on the playing fields. And with two PT classes a week and the afternoon games, you didn't need any more to go through all that hot-water-heating palaver involved in having a bath at home, at least until you left school and started thinking about girls.

Almost as soon as the term began, the blitzkrieg started and the school was evacuated to Weston-Super-Mare on the Bristol Channel. Some of the families, ours included, refused to let us go and the ones who stayed behind were split up among the schools which stayed open to teach these boys like us, boys whose families had elected to stay together. ("If a bomb *does* drop, our Ken's better off dead with us than being an orphan in one of those homes.") More of the younger boys stayed at home, and there were enough first- and second-formers to make up a class of each and these classes were sent to the local girls' school where we stayed for the next two years. (Another reason for not letting me be evacuated, not talked about except at home, was that my mum couldn't be sure I had the right manners yet. I didn't eat with my mouth open, but I did drink my tea with the spoon still in the cup until my sister stopped me. And apart from my table manners, there were all kinds of areas where I might betray my origins. How did other boys tell their parents that they were constipated? Had she taught me to get in the corners of my ears properly, with the face flannel? Weren't there kinds of food that had to be eaten in a special way? My mother had been concerned enough about behaving properly in the new world of Colliers Wood; she was even more wary of the world I had shot up to, so I wasn't evacuated.)

Ten

The Girls' School

WE VERY quickly acquired a distinct feeling that the Mitcham County School for Girls, though it was a county school and the parallel step for girls on the educational ladder, was superior to the boys' school. The war had not taken away their best teachers, of course, but it was also a question of tone, and of the physical plant and setting.

Inside the gates of the girls' school, there was a long drive edged on both sides with big plants with shiny dark green leaves, though in the early autumn there didn't seem to be any flowers. At the end of the drive the school faced the playing fields on one side and more bushes at the back, where we went in. The boys' school playing fields, on the other hand, had been laid out a long way from the school on a bit of waste ground where the dirt left over from tunnelling Morden station had been dumped and smoothed over, and to get to the playing field you cycled for a mile across Mitcham Common. The boys' school was surrounded by an asphalt area, much like Fortescue Road's playground, with a steel mesh fence separating it from an alley.

And the ambience of the girls' school was distinctly classier. We'd only been at the boys' school for a few weeks, but long enough to see that the girls' school dinners (called "lunch" in the girls' school) were not as good as ours. They went in a lot for fish pie and macaroni cheese and salads of wedges of slug-laden lettuce and pieces of tomato covered in "salad cream," while the boys were used to a fair number of meat pies and gravy, tastily seasoned by Mrs. Perry, the caretaker's wife, who knew what she was doing. The boys got cabinet pudding for afters, too, with custard, while the girls ate tapioca with a spoonful of jam in the middle, which when mixed together was christened "dragon-sperm" by a witty second-form boy.

But although the food was rotten, the service was clearly superior. Instead of lining up and being given a plate of food through a hatch, as in the boys' school, the girls were served by a prefect at the end of each table of eight, a senior girl to whom we passed our plates in turn. Then the prefect would lead us in conversation. Even the grace was different. Instead of "forwhatweareabouttoreceivemaytheLordmakeus-trulythankfulamen" bellowed from a raised podium at the end of the hall, followed by the clash of steel on a hundred and fifty plates, each girl prefect, when her table was ready, said a nun-like blessing, in Latin, and picked up her own tools as a signal for us to dig in. Our prefect was called Jean and she was thin, with dark hair caught up behind, terrifically feminine, with very white teeth that had a mother-of-pearl look about the front ones. She swelled gently, dove-like, under her gym tunic, and smelled of carnations. At the end of term she appeared one lunchtime in civilian dress, a blouse open enough so that when she leaned forward to hand you the soup you got a flash of breast, enough at twelve years to make me look at my soup in embarrassment. I had no desire to stroke her; I just wanted to kill on her behalf, animals if possible, people if necessary.

The boys were segregated into our own classes, a first form and a second form. Almost our first impression of the classroom in this new school was created by the geography mistress on the morning of day one. She walked in, sniffed the air, winced, and ordered the boys closest to the windows to open them wide. And that was before Munnings farted.

We understood perfectly what the geography mistress was saying, that we were from the element that smelled, unlike her girls. Munnings's instinctive response, "a voice from the gallery," as a wit named Kelly called it, was to give her something to complain about. (Later he said he never planned to let go such a ripsnorter; a short rasp-berry was what he was after.) The geography mistress could not ignore it, nor could she cope with it. She ran from the room and reappeared with one of the two masters we had brought with us from our own school. "I'll deal with this," he said and showed her to the door, clos-ing it behind her.

"Right," he said, rummaging through the desk and finding a plim-soll which he slapped against his palm. "Own oop now"—he was from Yorkshire—"Who made a disgoosting noise?"

No one spoke.

"Right, then. I shall have to take hostages. Coom up alphabetically, and bend over this chair." He banged the slipper on the desk. "You first, Atterbury. Oop you coom."

When Atterbury was in place, and the master was measuring the blow, like a golfer lining up a five-iron, Munnings said, "It was me."

"Aye. I thought you might break down. Not lost to all decency, I take it. Coom oop, then. Back to your seat, Atterbury." He waved the slipper about some more. "So, tell me, Munnings. Do you make dis-goosting noises at home, too?"

Munnings, seeing at that moment that the master was involved in something other than beating him—the man could barely keep from laughing—said, "No sir, it was an accident."

"In that case, it may not be all your fault. You may not be wicked, just not used to controlling yourself. Perhaps you're badly brought up. Is that it? Are you badly brought up?"

"Yes, sir."

"I'll tell Miss Haggard she was right, shall I? In the meantime we must make up for lost time. Learn to control ourselves. Coom round here." He led Munnings around the desk so that he was shielded from the view of Miss Haggard who was watching through the glass door. The slipper came down and we all winced but Munnings did not flinch. The master proceeded to pantomime five more ferocious strokes which bounced lightly off Munnings's bottom. "Right," he bellowed. "Get back to your place." He waggled the slipper at the door and at the face of the geography mistress, who now came in to the room, looking white at the terrible punishment she had caused to be inflicted on Munnings.

"You'll have no further trouble with this lot," our master said. "If you do, I'm just down the hall." He looked round the room, catching the eye of each boy in turn, lingering on Munnings, sending a message. Next time for keeps.

Munnings was incapable of restraining the spontaneous gesture. Music appreciation was taught by an enthusiastic twinkly little woman named Miss Dinn whom we liked, especially when she got all thirty of us proficient enough at the descant recorder to give a concert to the parents, with Kelly on piano. But that didn't stop Munnings from turning her piano into a barrel organ. He did it well. She was explaining the clever way Bach had put some piece of music together, and every time she played a few bars, Munnings, sitting at the end of the piano, out of sight of her but in full view of the class, turned the imaginary handle, stopping when she stopped, and even improvising a comic flourish in the style of Harpo Marx, looking amazed at the piano when she began to play before he had started to turn the handle, then giving a few quick turns to catch up, as it were.

Eventually, even our teacher realized something was going wrong as the class collapsed in hysterics, and then, the funniest moment of all, as she continued to play but looked around the corner of the piano to see what we were laughing at and saw Munnings, who was now playing the organ-grinder's monkey, holding out his cap to collect our change, enjoying himself so much he didn't notice he'd been rumbled.

This time the male teacher, who also liked Miss Dinn, was not amused. When she returned with him he hit Munnings so hard he lifted him out of his chair. When Munnings got to his feet, holding his ear, the master hit him through the door and they disappeared down the hall to the sound of Munnings's head being slapped.

If you were away for a day, you had to report to the headmistress the next morning with a note from your doctor or parent. I had had a day off with a cold and the next day I knocked on her door, was told to come in, entered, and handed her the note. As I turned to go, she said, "Come here."

In all the time we were there I never saw the woman smile and she was unsmiling now. "Come round here," she said, indicating the side of the desk. I went closer. "Show me your hands. Let me see your wrists. Now bend your head." She leaned over and looked inside my shirt collar. "Do you wash your neck every morning?" Her tone made it clear that it wasn't a real question.

"Yes."

"Not very well, I think."

Humiliation, rage, hatred. Did she think I didn't mind her insults? Wasn't I human? Was she running a workhouse? Would she have spoken to one of her girls like this? Or was this simply the natural way for a headmistress of a girls' county school to deal with a dirty little boy from the slums, the kind that had no feelings.

She gave me a problem. One way to show her what was what would have been to tell my mother, and let the headmistress feel the edge of the tongue of a respectable working-class woman who was trying to move us up in the world and was extremely sensitive to any charge that one of her kids had fallen short. She would have taken the headmistress's head off. The trouble was that she would have expected me to repeat what the headmistress had said in front of her and that would have meant . . . God knows what it would have led to. And there was the other certainty, that my mother would first make sure she was in the right, and I foresaw a scene in the bathroom with my mother, holding my head in the sink and scrubbing my whole body raw, in cold water and probably with a bit of pumice stone, before marching me back to the school and inviting the headmistress to inspect me from arsehole to breakfast-time. So I kept my mouth shut. All I did at the time was try to work on the right insult, the worst one I could think of. I looked for an answer in my experience, a reply we would make when some kid on the street told you you had a snotty nose. The right response was "And you've got a dirty bum." That's what my training taught me to say to someone who told me I had a dirty neck. I toyed with the idea of telling the other boys that I *had* said it, but they wouldn't have believed me. I enjoyed thinking it, though.

Two years later, in the middle of the war, when the Germans had given up trying to bomb the civilian population into submission, the rest of the school returned from Weston-Super-Mare and we reassembled on our own premises, but our two co-educational years made it difficult for some of us to settle down and readopt the culture of the boys' school. We returned to the "normal" world at a rebellious age—fourteen—having had a couple of years of the civilizing experience of pretty women (the prefects, mainly, though I was in love with the art mistress, too) and some good teaching. We were like the soldiers when they returned from the war, no longer willing to accept uncritically the values of a society we had swallowed whole in our young days, and beginning to develop the vocabulary to criticize it.

We found a focus for our discontent in the struggle to be allowed to continue to play soccer, the only field sport that could be adapted to the hockey pitches of the girls' school. The official sport was rugby, of course, the sport of the public schools that the county schools were trying to emulate. One of the virtues of making working-class boys play rugby was that it created a sharp separation between the world of the county school and the world most of the students came from. In the old world, most of them had been playing soccer since they could run, in the street with a tennis ball mainly, but you couldn't play rugby in the street, and no one tried.

An important difference between the two games is that soccer can be played and enjoyed by boys, and girls, who are neither talented nor physically impressive. Rugby, although it has its own skills, can also be played by the untalented, but it is a bruising game, and other things being equal, the bruisers have the advantage. Thus it was that Alan Simpson organized a petition and collected fifty names which he took to the headmaster in support of allowing soccer as an option to rugby. The petition was denied and the rebellion crushed in a single interview with the headmaster, who thus made outsiders of us all.

We didn't blame ourselves for hating rugby, as the misfits of previous generations might have done. We blamed rugby, and the school for offering it as socially superior to soccer, and we took some pride in refusing to play up and play the game. When we were forced to turn out for rugby, every Tuesday afternoon, a few of us took care to be picked last for the worst teams, and so were regarded with contempt by the keener boys, a contempt we reciprocated. By now Russia was in the war and socialists were agitating for a second front, an invasion of Europe to relieve the pressure on the eastern front. Communist sympathizers painted slogans on walls, demanding that we assist our Russian allies. Kelly, the class wit, joined us in not wanting to play rugby, or anything else, and kept on his woollen gloves and his overcoat even when picked for the seventh game, maintaining his identity by running up and down the touchline, shouting one of the Left's most popular slogans, "Strike now in the West and finish the job," whenever our team got the ball. (Kelly was the first person I ever heard use the response "I couldn't care less." That was in 1944. He was the class wit as well as the musician, like Oscar Levant.)

Another middle-class sport was cross-country running, so once a year we were made to run across Mitcham Common and back, with no previous practice or rehearsal or training, perhaps the dreariest effort to create a school spirit by means of athletics ever devised. The whole school ran, and the staff assembled at the finish line to cheer us home. They waited a long time to see some of us finish. As soon as we were out of sight of the school, our crowd turned it into a Sunday stroll, and made our way across the common chattering about soccer and the latest Bob Hope film, while being passed by smaller and smaller boys grimly responding to the spirit of the day. One bunch from the fifth form trotted briskly out of sight until they reached the first clump of bushes where they could safely stretch out for a smoke and a chat. You had to check in, though, so, late in the afternoon, the finishing line approaching, we broke into a trot, ironically aping the exhaustion of those who had arrived earlier.

This spirit of anti-establishmentarianism spread to other things— infected our lives, making us hostile to the brainwashing we were being subjected to. When we realized that we were being groomed to be middle-class supporters of the Conservative party, some of us became socialists. We used to mock the prefects with affected accents, accents they had adopted to assist them in their careers. One prefect we called Lord Haw-Haw because he sounded like the Nazi propagandist we listened to on the radio. No one we knew spoke like that. We watched each other for signs that we were succumbing to their culture and jeered at any conscious vowel-shift we overheard. At the same time, the system was performing its silent ministry, and while we were quick to jump on accents we felt had been acquired too easily and from too far up the ladder, already none of my cronies shared the same vowels as their fathers. The scholarship examination was doing its work. Within two years, Robbie and I were strangers.

In the area of manners appropriate to a young gentleman, the school carried on where Mr. Thomas and my sister had left off. So Dickey Bird, our English master, now gave us a lesson on how to manage our knives and forks. ("The tines of the fork always pointing down, unless you shift your fork into the other hand when you may reverse it; bread to be broken, never cut—cutting is for the French and Americans . . .") We laughed but I was grateful for the advice, then and later, because I had more to learn than most, in spite of what May had shown me. Even to flout the rules (if you had the courage) you needed to know them.

They did not actually give us lessons in elocution, but we all knew from the first day to pronounce our aitches. Some of us were better at faking it than others: a boy called Churcher who later became my pal was sneered at in front of the class for having the wrong accent by Gaffer Cook, an old man who was hired to teach history. When Cook asked Churcher where he learned to speak like that, Churcher made the mistake of telling him, and Cook made fun of him, poncing about in the front of the classroom, saying, "'Ackney, sir. I'm from 'Ackney," to make the creepers laugh.

Afterwards, when Churcher and I became mates, he told me he really came from Bethnal Green, but he had only said Hackney because he thought it sounded better, a subtlety well beyond Gaffer Cook.

One of our troubles was that the war had taken away our role models. All the healthy young male teachers had disappeared into the armed forces, and their replacements were a mixed lot, some of them untrained women. One, Jesse Jewett, was the best history teacher I have ever had, and we were lucky to keep our maths teacher, Mr. Stevens: he was past retirement but he stayed on for the "Emergency." The others we just put up with. English was a subject that I could teach myself. Although there were only two books in our house—one was by Ouida, and the other was a Richmal Crompton "William" book with most of the pages torn out and the rest scribbled on—I was now borrowing ten books a week from the public library, using cards which I made my family apply for. I wish I could have taught myself French, Latin, science, geography, woodwork, music, and art, in all of which I had a lot of trouble. Part of the trouble was that I had discovered the cult of the amateur, that if a thing was difficult it wasn't worth doing. Only English and history were easy. And there was no one at home or at school perceptive enough to smack my head for being such an affected little twerp, or even to point out what I was really doing.

Many of the new teachers were not teachers by training or vocation but former travel agents and such, and sometimes a teacher would go missing, unable to face us any more. We had four geography teachers one year, refugees from Hitler mostly, including one who was said to be an Estonian diplomat, who told us stories about the countries he had lived in. One substitute geography teacher shrieked at us continually to use some initiative. It was his favourite word, and he used it at least once in every class, getting on our nerves until someone hit on the notion of privately substituting the word "shit" for "initiative." It was exactly the right level of gag for our age. "Sir, how shall I attach the map to my essay when I hand it in?" "Oh, use a bit of initiative," came the invariable reply. We rolled about in hysterics, leaving him blinking, mystified.

Between teachers, the headmaster sometimes filled in himself. This gave him a chance to show how teaching should be done. For a couple of classes he would improvise talks that were lively and entertaining, but he soon became bored and then a prefect would appear to keep us quiet while we did our own thing, under the guise of "reading ahead."

That headmaster was something of a showman, and every year he produced a very enjoyable Gilbert and Sullivan operetta which most of us sang in. I would have admired him more if he had not given off the air of having come down in the world in heading Mitcham County School, as he probably had. I had almost no contact with him in the time I was there until right at the end, when he told my mother that I should regard myself as lucky to have been there at all.

One day he went round the school, speaking to each class during the period set aside for religious instruction. Hands behind his back, going up and down on his toes, he said, "Piss, shit, fuck, arsehole, prick, cum—these are the words you have scratched on the walls of the latrine to illustrate the cave drawings you have engraved. As you see, there's nothing clever about knowing these words. I know them. Everyone does. But it is not the kind of language to be expected at a school like this. The latrines will be repainted in the holidays. Any boy caught defacing the walls in future will be caned and expelled, back to the gutter where he belongs."

Mouthing all those rude words was only a bit of showmanship, as we could see at the time, but we were struck dumb. Such language we only heard when the pubs turned out, certainly not in the gutter outside our homes, and never indoors. We had seen the words, of course, written on lavatory walls, put there, we believed, by the local kids who used the school yard at night after the government took the iron railings away to melt them down for munitions. We were embarrassed, then, not *by* the headmaster, but *for* him, a fully grown man using language like that in front of a class of young boys.

Eleven

The Blitz

THE WAR itself, though it affected our education, hardly interfered with our lives. Brothers and sisters went off and came back on leave. Len went into the navy after conducting a long campaign of non-violent resistance to the authorities who wanted him to stay in the munitions factory, a job classified as essential to the war effort which exempted him from military service. But Len had heard the call of the sea and stayed in bed until they agreed to let him heed it. They refused for a long time, and he refused to go to work at the munitions factory. He engaged in, for me, a wearisome campaign to get the authorities to give up. I shared a bedroom with him, and every morning I was awakened by the sound of my mother calling from the next room, "Len! Len! You up?"

"All right, all right. I'm up."

Two or three minutes later. "Len! Len! Are you up?"

Then I, who did not have to get up for another hour, chimed in from the other bed, "Len! Len! Get up! She's not going to stop. Come on. Get up!"

"Who do you think you are? Sod off!"

Then, "Len! Len! You up yet?"

On and on until she came in with a saucepan of cold water. "You want this poured over you? Get up!"

"Oh, bloody hell, all right." And he would get up, but not necessarily to go to work. From time to time two men in raincoats would appear, looking for him, because he had not been to the factory for a week. They explained to my mother that he could go to prison for refusing to do war work. This appalled my mother. Trouble with the law was what she thought she had left behind in Kennington.

"Speak to him, Jack," she exhorted my father when he came home from work. "Make him mind."

"He won't mind me. You see."

He didn't. The men in raincoats came back and found Len at home. They tried the same threats that had frightened my mother.

"What's so important about me doing war work?" Len wanted to know.

"Because it's vital, son."

"Yeah? You do it then, you look strong enough. A cripple could do your job. I want to go into the navy. Defend my country, like."

In the end they gave in, as Len, advised by his mates who were more in tune with the realities of the wartime world than my mother, knew they would. Why put a bloke in prison who wants to go in the navy? Makes no sense. Be in all the papers.

He spent the rest of the war on a minesweeper in the North Sea, under Mad Jack, as Len christened him, a former trawler skipper. The minesweeper had been converted from a trawler by mounting a single machine-gun above the deck. The purpose of this gun was to be able to make some response to attacking aircraft, but according to Len, Mad Jack saw it as an assault weapon with which he attacked German minelayers. He prowled the North Sea, looking for vessels to shoot at, or, Len suspected, ram, if they were too big.

I think Len wanted to get into the navy because it had a more convivial image than the other services. The air force was full of "Brylcreem Boys," so called after the hair cream they were supposed to affect, and gave them a slightly prettified image to Len and his mates. The image of the army, on the other hand, came to him through our father—stories of a life in the trenches, waiting in the mud to go "over the top" and meet a lot of Germans drunk on schnapps, carrying bayonets. But the navy's image was of "Jolly Jack" the sailor, a couple of weeks at sea with a gang of pals, then ashore into the arms of the girls who were waiting on the dock at every port. I thought they would reject him because he couldn't swim, but that turned out not to be a qualification.

So I got a bedroom to myself, except when someone came home on leave. In fact, the war saved me from the embarrassment of being part of such a large family. I had sisters as old as most people's mothers, and under normal circumstances I would have been sharing a bed with at least one brother, and probably two. As it was, with all my brothers in the services, three of my sisters married, and one in the Women's Auxiliary Air Force, there was just me and one older and one younger sister, which meant I got Joe's old room, the tiny box room, all to myself, just like my school friends. Had there been no war, I would never have taken a friend home because of the stories he would have carried back about the way we lived.

At the beginning of the war, if the alert sounded, we lay down under the dining-room table, and slept there until the all-clear. A few people, noticing that when a house got a direct hit sometimes only the stair-case survived, took to sitting under the stairs during a raid, but there wasn't room for all of us under the stairs, and you couldn't stay there all night. Grandma Wright in Westminster had died, and soon after my grandfather was bombed out of his rooms and came to live with us.

He died one night early in the blitz, peacefully in his bed, while we were still sleeping under the table. My father crept downstairs to let my mother know. "Daisy," he said, in a large whisper, "he's gorn."

"Gorn? Gorn where?"

"Gorn!"

"How was I supposed to know? Creeping down here, saying, 'He's gorn!' like that. All right. Don't wake everybody up. I'll see to it in the morning."

But we were awake, and giggling. We replayed the scene often, creeping in on each other (when my mother was elsewhere) to whisper, "Daisy, he's gorn." "Gorn where?" *"Gorn!"*

During the blitz, many of our neighbours slept in the nearby Underground station, a natural air-raid shelter, but there was as much chance of getting my mother to go down there, among a lot of strangers, as there was of getting her to camp out in Piccadilly Circus, and we spent the nights in our own Anderson shelter. This was a corrugated-steel affair issued by the government to be erected in the backyard. It came in sections, which, when bolted together, formed a small hut with a curved roof, about seven feet long, five feet wide, and high enough in the centre for a man to stand upright in. There was an open entrance at one end. The head of the house was supposed to dig a pit three or four feet deep and set the shelter in it, then cover the hut with a foot or so of earth as additional protection. A hole about three feet square and two feet deep was then dug in front of the entrance. To get into the shelter, you had to step down into this hole, stoop, then step down the remaining distance. Inside, four bunks were attached to the walls, two on each side. Once ours was built my mother and my sisters had the lower bunks, Jean sharing a bunk with Doris, and Len and I had the upper. My father stayed in the house, because he preferred to sleep under his own roof, in his own bed.

Some of the handier neighbours lined their shelters with concrete, built blast walls of brick in front of their doorways, and even made little flights of steps down to the shelters. They often fitted up the interiors with shelves and lights to make them more comfortable, and the more elaborately finished shelters were as compact and self-contained as one-room apartments.

Ours was not one of these. My father still had none of the suburban skills of his neighbours. That the shelter was erected at all was a miracle. Digging the hole was no problem—my father was probably the strongest man on the street—but after that he was just guessing. He piled up a small hill of earth and rocks in place of a blast wall, and never bothered about steps. He put an apple box inside the shelter to step down on, and hung a piece of sacking over the doorway. In wet weather, the approach became one long, greasy slope. I used to go first and help my mother and sisters from inside. Sometimes I literally caught them, like a playground director at the foot of a children's slide. The floor was rude earth, and as a result of faulty measuring the shelter was never quite straight, so that it looked as though it had been through one bombardment already. My mother had no real faith in it. She was convinced that her husband had made such a mess of putting it up that it was useless, and the only reason she stayed in it was because she did not want to show my father up in front of the neighbours.

When dusk came, other families along the street trooped down their garden paths with flashlights, wireless sets, cards, dominoes, books, vacuum flasks, and all the other stuff they needed for a cosy evening, but for us, dusk meant total extinction for the night. When it rained, there was two inches of water and mud on the floor, and we climbed immediately into the bunks. My mother stretched a piece of wood across the space between the two lower bunks, on which she kept a candle and her purse. For a while, we relied on the one candle for illumination. Then some local Milquetoast told her that a candle used up all the oxygen, and after that our evenings were spent in darkness, my young sister and I playing an imaginary game of I Spy (we couldn't spy anything except the corrugated iron over our heads), and my mother trying to remember if she had turned off the gas stove. On really wet nights, when the water was a foot deep, I took a few pebbles to bed with me, because it was fun to drop them over the edge of the bunk and hear the *ploomp* they made in the dark waters below.

My dad would see us safely into the shelter, and then go back to the house to sleep. The idea of him asleep at the top of the house used to drive my mother mad. Not only was he a really sound sleeper, but because of his practice of piling three or four overcoats on top of the bedcovers to keep out the cold and the incidental noise of the raids, it took a specially heavy anti-aircraft barrage to get through to him. My mother used to fret about that. At the height of a raid, she would sit up in her bunk. "Listen to that. *Listen* to it," she would urge us. "The whole place being blown to bits and that bloody man asleep upstairs! *He* doesn't care."

This wasn't quite true. There was an anti-aircraft gun a few hundred feet from the house, and when this started up, my father would usually wake up with a guilty conscience, knowing that my mother was also awake, and angry. He would immediately hurry downstairs and make a cup of tea, and a few minutes later the sacking over our entrance would be pulled back, and there he would be, whispering hoarsely (so as not to wake the children), "Daisy! Daisy! Are you all right? I brought you a cup of tea."

The sky behind him would be a blaze of searchlights and shellbursts and, once, a flaming barrage balloon, and my mother would grab the tea. "All right? All *right*? Course I'm all right. Go back inside. What's the matter with you? You gone daft? Go inside!" And the sacking would fall into place again as my father returned to bed.

Eventually he got a job as nightwatchman in his own stables in Kennington, one of the most heavily bombed parts of the City. That way he could sleep at home during the day, when there weren't many air raids, and it was less nerve-racking keeping the horses calm during a raid than trying to assure my mother both that he was safe and that he knew it was dangerous to be outside. My young sister and I missed him a lot. We used to enjoy those visits, when the lifted cloth gave us a glimpse of the fireworks outside. For us, the whole terrible struggle was reduced to a familiar domestic argument—a kind of storm in which my father didn't have enough sense to get out of the rain.

The war wasn't nearly as important to me as the ordinary life at school. The only actual war incident I was part of happened one night when I answered a knock at the door to find a tramp there with three days' growth of beard and a sack on his back. Because of the blackout regulations I had to draw the curtain behind me before I opened the door wide, so there was no light for enemy bombers to see me by. The street lights were out, of course, and there was no moon or stars, so he was indistinguishable, too.

"Ullo, son," he said, and smiled.

It was as frightening as the appearance of Magwitch in David Lean's film version of *Great Expectations* but I stood my ground and asked him what he wanted. "I want to come in," he said.

And then, just as he was telling me, my mother came into the passage to find out what was going on and reacted with a scream, "O Gawd, it's Ron," and pushed past me to let him in.

Ron's ship, part of a Murmansk convoy, had been sunk near Archangel, but he had been rescued and taken ashore in Russia. In time, he joined a home-going convoy and returned to a survivors' camp in Scotland. The survivors were supposed to recuperate until they were fit to be seen by the civilian population, but Ron, being Ron, just walked out of the camp and hitchhiked home.

My mother fed him most of the food in the house, which he ate while she heated the water for a bath, and he washed himself and went to bed for sixteen hours, then got up and ate the rest of our week's rations and went back to bed for another eight hours. Then he had to go back to Scotland.

After that he went on the Atlantic run, on oil tankers, but he survived the U-boats and came home safely.

After Dunkirk, Joe was sent to Greece in time to cover the retreat of the fighting troops, and moved on to take part in the evacuation of Crete. Once again he found himself part of the rearguard covering the embarkation of the Welsh Guards or some such crack regiment, and found a place on one of the last landing craft to leave the beach. From here he went to Libya to be fattened up for the next battle.

Mad Jack repeatedly tried to get Len drowned in the North Sea but Len survived like his brothers. Gladys came as close as any of them to not coming home when she was machine-gunned on a Bournemouth street by a stray German aircraft. She escaped by lying in the gutter, as she had been instructed.

And then, one day, while we were in class, Mr. Gush, the French master, was called to the door of the classroom to hear something from the headmaster. When he returned he looked solemn but happy. "This morning," he said (in French), "the Allied armies crossed the Channel and landed on the beaches of Normandy. At this moment they are fighting to secure a beachhead. The second front has begun."

There was a breathless hush, mainly because even after four years of French classes, we couldn't understand what he was saying. He made the announcement again, more slowly, emphasizing the key words, pointing to a map of France on the wall to indicate where the troops had landed, and miming the firing of a sten gun until we got it. It was probably the most momentous announcement of the war for a group of fifteen-year-olds, many of whom had fathers or brothers who would be involved. We knew it meant the beginning of the end.

For the civilians, nothing much more happened until the V-1 bombs appeared on the scene. These "buzz bombs" sometimes approached before the sirens could give warning, but you could tell roughly where a V-1 would land from its position in the sky when the engine cut out. One sunny afternoon, I was playing soccer in the rec when one of them appeared. We ran to shelter, and I saw it dip and heard the roar of the explosion, which came from the direction of our house. I raced home and found the house a shambles; the blast had taken out most of the windows, and tiles from the roof were strewn across the street. My mother was already at work trying to clean up the mess. I started to help when she suddenly screamed, "Your dad— he's upstairs!" Running up to the bedroom, we plunged into a choking cloud of plaster dust which had fallen on the bed, covering it completely. We tore off the mess of plaster and laths, which seemed about a foot thick, and when we eventually uncovered my father we found him dazed but not unconscious. My mother immediately assumed he had slept through the whole business (he *looked* as though he had), and she collapsed, sitting down on the bed, in tears for the first time I had seen her, but also furious, blaming him for the fright his appearance had given her.

Twelve

Leaving School

LIKE EVERYONE else over the age of ten, I had to earn my own
pocket money, and I had a morning paper round during the first year
of the blitz. The papers had to be delivered between the end of the
raids, after the all-clear had sounded, and getting ready for school. This
was the best time for picking up shrapnel from the anti-aircraft shells,
some of it still warm to the touch. Later in the war, shrapnel fell out
of favour as a souvenir because it got rusty too quickly. A brand new
gleaming piece of twisted metal would start to rust in a day or two and
soon lose its attraction. The best finds were the brass nose-cones, and
on one gala morning I found three. Sometimes, after a bombing, you
couldn't deliver all your papers because the police would be clearing up
an area that had been hit, but there wasn't much damage on my round.
Ray Hampton found a whole house missing one morning when he
tried to deliver a paper. The front door was still there, he said, but there
was nothing round it or behind it, just a gap in the street with a door
frame and a door.

I only delivered papers for a year. When I stopped, my father
assumed I was lazy, a quitter, made soft by too much "eddication." (I
had got out of a warm bed every morning in one of the coldest win-

ters of the age and shivered my way round the dark streets without missing a single day for nine months, but that didn't count. Eventually my "quitter" streak showed through, just as he suspected it would.) It wasn't true. I just couldn't face the medical again. Boys who wanted to deliver papers had to be examined every year by a doctor to certify that they were fit to do the job. The doctors examined our chests for signs of tuberculosis, and felt the walls of our abdomens to make sure we didn't have a hernia. So, before I could start my round, a woman doctor listened to my chest with a stethoscope and then unbuckled my trousers and fumbled with my balls as if they were made of steel like those sold in Chinese novelty shops for reducing stress. She took a very long time to establish what she was looking for and sure enough, by the time she was finished, I had my first externally activated non-spontaneous erection, though the cause wasn't sex but friction and embarrassment. It soon faded but it was a real horn while it lasted, and my face was black with shame as I tried to step away. But she hung on gamely, saying, "It's all right," fumbling away for several more seconds before she let me go. "It's perfectly natural," she said, tapping me lightly on the head with her pencil and smiling.

For her, maybe, because she knew nothing about the way it was in Colwood Gardens, but not for me. I might have had to stay away from women doctors for the rest of my life, but I told Robbie when I saw him and he set me straight, told me it would have happened to anybody; he thought he might try to get a paper route himself, he grinned, but there were no vacancies. But a year later, I could not bring myself to be examined again, or tell my parents why I was quitting the paper route, so I had to get a job working all day Saturday in a banana factory, a dark steamy warehouse where bananas were ripened, to earn some money. (I got six shillings a week for the paper round, including the Saturday morning collection, a sum hard to replace.) It meant giving up my free time with my mates, but I had no choice.

Bombs killed two boys I knew, one only fifty yards from our house as he was cycling home for his Sunday dinner.

I was frightened once in the Underground when the train stopped, the lights went out, and some fool shouted that the tunnel was flooded.

And once, walking home from school, having spent my bus fare on toffee, I passed two old women on Western Road, near the gasworks, as one was saying to the other, "A landmine, they say, and if it goes orf, it'll take you, me, the gasworks, and most of Mitcham with it. Could go any minute. Come on." And they scuttled off down a side road. There was no one else about and I ran like hell, expecting any second to be plucked out of my clothes and deposited a mile away, naked and dead. (Those same two old women, or two very much like them, appeared several times later in my life. Once I came home from school to find them drinking tea with my mother. That time, after learning who I was, they looked at me closely, and one said to my mother, "I don't think he'll make old bones, Daisy." Often they waited for me on street corners, going silent as I approached, then watching me, shaking their heads as I walked past them and on down the road. They could tell I had been up to something.)

Otherwise, the war, for a schoolboy, was the background; the foreground was school.

In the summer of 1944 the school pitched some tents on a farm near Cheddar in Somerset and we helped to get in the harvest. I was fifteen now, and becoming aware of passages. Two of my cronies, Ray Hampton (now known as Hambone) and Bert Churcher (newly christened Peastick by us because he was tall and thin) had left school, both of them believing that life had to be more interesting and pleasanter elsewhere, and that made me aware that school would not go on for ever. Hambone said later that the stay at the girls' school had spoiled him. It was altogether a more civilized environment than the boys' school—the physical setting, the teaching, and the agreeableness of the senior girls who we found out afterwards had been asked to mentor us. Hambone got lucky and was looked after by Lucy, who we were all soft on. As for Peastick, when we returned to the boys' school he was separated from all his friends and put into a different form for no good reason, so it was like his first week of school all over again. And Hambone and Peastick hated rugger as much as any of us.

I understood why they went, and I was sorry because they were both cronies of mine now and would be hard to replace. But I didn't feel tempted to join them. I had begun to feel apprehensive about the future, which seemed to promise nothing, and I began to take some responsibility for my performance at school. I began to wonder, prompted into it by a new friend, Stan Yass, whether if I did some work, I might become a student, and I found the idea attracted me slightly. It was almost too late, but I set myself a couple of small academic tasks and achieved them. I thought about the sixth form, admiring a boy who had decided at the last minute to study languages and set himself the task of learning School Certificate Latin in one year. I could do that, I thought, if I took myself seriously, though perhaps not in Latin.

The closeness of living six to a tent in the harvest camp brought out the beginnings of a tolerance for each other which we were old enough to allow, an awareness of the sheer interestingness of boys whom I had dismissed as drips for the last four years. The old cliques broke up and were replaced by new friendships, some of them enduring. We worked in the fields, stooking, haymaking, and, if we could not avoid it, thinning root crops, the most back-breaking work of all. We worked alongside Italian prisoners of war, surely the most pleasant enemies any country ever had, or so it seemed to us. They had no money, so many of them turned to making things they could sell, women's jackets out of old blankets, and wallets and purses from scraps of leather. The Italian war effort had collapsed and Italy was about to surrender and some of the prisoners were beginning to wonder if they would not be better off staying in England than returning to a ravaged homeland. In the end, they all had to go back, and I put one of them in a book forty years later when I needed an Italian peasant with a fair command of English. All of the prisoners we worked with seemed to speak English fluently.

In 1945, as the final victory in Europe approached, so did the School Certificate examinations. I still led the class in English, and history and mathematics had remained interesting enough, but nothing else did; no one made me work hard. I had no self-discipline (my father was right about that). In spite of feeling the beginnings of a desire to achieve something, I was heading for ignominy. But that new friend, Stanley Yass, the only Jewish boy in the school, now took me seriously in hand.

Stan was not in my form but in the rival form, 5B. I had noticed him in the air-raid shelters when roll was being called to make sure the whole class had transferred from school to shelter intact. There was another boy in 5B at the end of the alphabet, a boy named Yapp, and Yass and Yapp entertained each other and their classmates by replying to the roll with each other's names: "Yapp?"—"Yass," then "Yass?"—"Yapp." I heard it in the shelter for the first time and thought it hilarious.

Stan was the first boy I had met who worked hard to get B grades who wasn't a drip. Stan said, "If you don't get your School Certificate, you'll be a bus conductor." I hadn't thought about it like that. I applied myself a little, just in time, and got my School Certificate with failures in art and music and Latin, but enough other passes to scrape by, including a distinction in English literature.

The same headmaster assembled us all in one room to hear the results. To put us out of our misery quickly, he had memorized the important result, whether we had passed or failed, and rapidly ran round the room saying, "Passed, passed, failed . . ." etc., to a lot of boys, some of whom he hardly knew. It was a tricky performance because he must have taken some trouble to memorize us by our faces, and he meant well.

I had passed. Then he read out how we had done in individual subjects, going slowly round the room and I was in agony to confirm the mark in one subject. When he came to me, he looked at the marks and stopped, puzzled. He knew me well enough because I had been a policeman in his *Pirates of Penzance*. Then he read out the English mark—"A." There was a note of slight doubt in his voice.

"That's right," I said, a bit too quickly. I knew it was coming—the exam had been a piece of cake—and his pause made me belligerent. He looked down at the marks to be sure, and looked at me again, before he moved on. I had distinguished myself for the first time in my life, in however small a way, and congratulations were in order. But he just looked at me, thoughtfully, and moved on.

It was a bleak period. I did not seem to have felt as much of an outsider within the school as Peastick or Hambone, although there was no chance of that headmaster's ever choosing me as a prefect, because I certainly lacked the right attitude; for him, I was what was wrong with the school, perhaps he found me common. But, probably, fear of the world outside, perhaps some slight encouragement by Dickey Bird, the English master, a small genuine desire to remain a student—all of these combined as I offhandedly, casually, mentioned to my mother that Derek Ockenden and Len Dunkley, two of my school friends whom she knew and admired, were continuing on to the sixth form with the idea of going to university.

"You can put that out of your head," she snapped. "Right now. You've already been allowed to stay in school far longer than anyone else and now it's time to start paying it back."

I had not expected or deserved anything else. For her, I was one of the lucky ones, but all good things had to end. I couldn't lay in front of her or the rest of my family a burning ambition to be or do something that required more training or education. My one area of excellence seemed valueless, like being good at music appreciation. I had no mentors or advisors except Stan, and he was being apprenticed to a quantity surveyor. Fortunately even this was outside my reach, because the weekly stipend for a student in the minor professions—surveying, accountancy, and such—was intended only as pocket money, making even this level of qualification unavailable to someone who had to pay his own way from now on. I say *fortunately* because otherwise I might have been thwarted when I did finally become seized with an irresistible ambition to take ship somewhere.

It was time to leave. The sadness that always accompanies the end of an academic year was made more intense by the knowledge that this was the last. I had no affection for the school, but I was not looking forward to the future. I needed a job, and I couldn't think of anything I wanted to do. Before I started work, there was one last summer of harvest camp. They pitched our tents on Viscount Cowdray's estate near Midhurst in Sussex, and we swam in the pool of Midhurst Grammar. Midhurst was a distinctly superior school to Mitcham County in every way, but the war temporarily allowed for some fraternization among classes, here as elsewhere, though the viscount kept his distance. It was the custom to swim naked at Midhurst Grammar; the summer was very hot and we had a fine time aping our betters in that pool, as, I suppose, did that old master, a naturalist, he called himself, who sat naked, sunning himself in a corner of the wall surrounding the pool, watching us play in the water, smiling.

One day I had an appointment in the headmaster's study, along with my mother, for a five-minute counselling session which would settle the rest of my life. I sat there, ashamed of my mother for being a shabby little woman with a cockney accent, and hating the headmaster for knowing it, and for having trained me to be ashamed, and furious with her for whispering to me loudly, "Say, 'Sir,'" every time I spoke to him, as she had been doing since I was five.

He had a list of job vacancies and from that he suggested two, both clerkships, one with the United Dairies Company, and the other with the Asiatic Petroleum Company. The choice was easy: the petroleum company had its offices in the City of London, whereas the milk company had its offices in the next suburb. I was very keen both to sample the London I was already reading about in novels, and to get out of Colliers Wood as much and as often as I could.

Thirteen

London

IN COLLIERS WOOD, in 1945, clerkships at the Asiatic Petroleum Company were reckoned to be good jobs, available only to those with School Certificates. A medical was necessary because you had to join the pension fund, and a bank account so your salary (not wages) could be paid into it, monthly. Bank accounts were very rare in Colliers Wood; when the county council awarded me a grant of two guineas a term to subsidize the cost of my school uniform, it came in the form of a cheque which was uncashable without a bank account, so we had to take it to the corner grocery shop, Rendell's, and spend some of it on milk and bread and tea. This was standard practice: no one else we knew had a bank account, except Vi, of course, for The George, but she only visited us about once a month, and The George was too far for one of us to go just to cash a cheque. Some people had Post Office savings accounts, but in our family any surplus money was kept in cash, in my mother's purse. My father kept his personal savings in one-pound notes in a shopping bag in the wardrobe.

So getting a bank account, and a chequebook (and paying a stamp tax on every withdrawal) was pretty heady stuff. It was also absurd. My salary was a hundred and sixty pounds a year, paid monthly. In terms of paying the rent, buying a season ticket on the Underground, and so on, I lived weekly, so I had to be very careful to get fifty-two weeks' expenses out of twelve paycheques, by allowing for two or three extra days in every cheque, except February. In practice, on the day they deposited my salary into my account, I, along with most of the other junior employees of the Asiatic Petroleum Company, lined up, wrote a cheque, and drew it all out. I then lived carefully for three weeks and was impoverished for the rest of the month.

I used to think that the only possible reason for paying our money into a bank account, rather than giving us cheques, was to show us how we had come up in the world by joining the Asiatic Petroleum Company. The working class got wages and kept their savings in the Post Office; the genteel classes, including the lower middle class which I had now joined, earned salaries and kept their money in bank accounts. But any real workers I knew—plumbers, bricklayers, and so on—regarded my little salary as a joke, and the fact that it was paid monthly they saw as a swindle to rob me of four weeks' pay a year. Their unions wouldn't have stood for it. But the real reason, of course, was that it was more convenient for the Asiatic Petroleum Company, and we didn't have a union to complain to.

I was the office boy in the insurance department. No attempt was made to interest me in insurance, or to train me in any way whatever. As a sixteen-year-old, I was marking time until I did my two years of national service, which would begin at eighteen. There was no point in training me until that was finished, so I, along with all other sixteen-year-olds, faced the prospect of kicking my heels for four years until life started properly. The position was so empty of any interest or challenge that it performed the useful function of leaving me free to daydream and discover in myself a determination, when I finished my national service, to avoid any future involving the Asiatic Petroleum Company or any company like it. Mostly, along with two or three other office boys, I spent my time plotting how to get away. The army would be my first escape. After that I would see.

In the meantime the social struggle continued. It was just as necessary to conceal one's origins around Bishopsgate as it had been at school. Some of the juniors in other departments had actually been to minor public schools, and some others sounded as if they had. You were expected to wear a suit and a tie from Monday to Friday; on Saturday mornings you could wear a sports jacket and grey flannel trousers and a tie. Fortunately clothing was rationed, so there was plenty of excuse for shabbiness, but you had to observe the forms. One Saturday, one of the older office boys in another department visited me in the insurance department, wearing a parody of an overcoat with wide lapels and a pinched waist that looked like the costume for a stage bookmaker. It must have been handed down to him by a flashy uncle. Nobody said anything to his face, but one of the older men in my department, who should have known better, thought he was being very witty by singing, apparently to himself, the first lines of "Knocked 'Em in the Old Kent Road." ("Last night, down our alley came a toff/Great, big, geezer wiv an 'acking cough . . .") The boy was a pal of mine, so I didn't laugh, but I didn't encourage him to hang about in the office, either.

The world of sports continued to sort us out. Many of those who had played rugby at school continued to play in Old Boys clubs, and the sports club of the Asiatic Petroleum Company fielded its own teams. I, alone among my peers at the office, was a football fan, specifically a fanatical Chelsea supporter. I would not have actually denied being a Chelsea supporter if an office colleague had asked me; I simply didn't brag about belonging once a week to the cloth-cap brigade, even though Chelsea supporters were in the upper ranks of football society.

I had supported Chelsea for as long as I could remember, ever since Joe had taken me to a game when I was about seven or eight. By the time I was fourteen, and in full opposition to the rugby crowd at school, I was cheering from the terraces of Stamford Bridge every other Saturday afternoon. When I first started going, the war was on, and a lot of players from other teams who were now in the services were temporarily joining local teams where they happened to be stationed. Sometimes the difficulty of fielding a full side was so acute that clubs had to appeal to the crowd on the terraces for able-bodied players to help out for the afternoon. I was hoping the war would last ten more years so that I could step forward, because I had not yet admitted to myself that I was really no good at all at the thing I most enjoyed doing besides reading.

Thus my heroes included George Hardwick, who came from Middlesborough, and played for England; and Charlie Mitten, from Manchester, I think; and many other imports. But the greatest player of all, more revered by me than the great Stanley Matthews himself, was Tommy Walker, the Scottish international inside right, whom even at that age I would cheerfully have followed into battle. The afternoon when Tommy Walker led Chelsea in an 11–2 victory over Crystal Palace was, up to that point, the happiest afternoon of my life. Never mind the lopsided score, which reflected the play; the afternoon was a ninety-minute demonstration by Walker of what you can do with a football. Most of the people who rave about the later demonstration that Stanley Matthews put on against the Russians (which was brilliant, I was there, I wouldn't dream of denying it) do not think anyone else could have done it. I think Tommy Walker could have.

Since I only began watching football during the war, I assumed that the conditions under which it was played were normal, that is, that the teams were divided into northern and southern divisions. But this was a temporary arrangement designed to cut down on travel. When, after the war, the old leagues (or some form of them) were resumed, I discovered that the war had obscured the football league's own class system, that my team had been playing some very lower-class clubs like Millwall, Charlton Athletic, and Brentford (especially Brentford) simply because the war had made it necessary. These were third division clubs which properly played among themselves, except once a year when they were given a chance in the Football Association Cup (if they survived the first two rounds) to play a game with aristocrats like Chelsea and Arsenal. The Football Association also relieved the social pressure by providing a minimal form of upward mobility in the league play; at the end of the season two clubs were promoted into the class above and two demoted, but the records show that if any of the real aristocrats like Chelsea slipped, it was usually only for a season or two.

Much of this has changed. Wimbledon is now in the premier division. In those days I would have as soon expected to see Tooting and Mitcham there.

There was no money. I had to contribute to the house, and pay my fare to the office, and I was left with about a pound a week to spend. During the day I wore shoes with pieces of linoleum in them to keep out some of the rainwater. I owned one office shirt with two collars which I changed (the collars—the shirt I kept on all week) on Wednesday or Thursday, depending on what I was doing at night. I went without gloves in winter because I couldn't afford a pair of leather ones and woollen ones marked you as a weed. And so on. But at night, for the first three weeks of the month, it was another thing. How could we carve out our nights from the scraps left from days lived like this?

Like this: the Asiatic Petroleum Company supplied luncheon, free, three courses—typically, Windsor soup and bread, toad-in-the-hole (sausages baked in Yorkshire pudding) with potatoes and cabbage, cabinet pudding with custard, and coffee. A free lunch from the employer was standard in those days and formed an important addition to the food rations; if an employer was too small to have their own dining room and kitchen, then they supplied luncheon vouchers, worth half a crown, to be spent in any restaurant which honoured them, as most did. Free luncheons made it possible to stay in town after work for the evening, because if we ate as much as possible at lunch (if you went to the last sitting, you could sometimes get seconds of the cabinet pudding), and brought sandwiches from home for dinner, all we needed was the price of a cup of tea to wash the sandwiches down. Tuppence. Then your season ticket on the Underground, which got you to work and home, also covered most of your travelling at night. You might have to pay three ha'pence to buy a ticket to get you past the turnstile but, then as now, once on the platform no one could tell where you had come from, so you could get home free.

I set aside ten shillings for Saturdays—football and the Saturday night dance—and spent the rest on theatres, concerts, and cinemas. You could get into the galleries of a lot of theatres for a shilling, and you could get into the upper circle of Covent Garden Opera House for half a crown. From here I first saw *Rigoletto* and *La Bohème*, and got angry at the money I had wasted on some Wagner rubbish. But most of all, from here I had a musical experience the like of which I have never had since. The opera was *La Traviata*, the company, the San Carlos Opera Company, and the singer was Margherita Carosio, whom I have never heard since. That night, when I was sure there were to be no more curtain calls, I rushed around to the stage door to get as close as I could when she came out. She appeared from the stage door, looked frightened at the mob of faces, said, "Please," in a soft little voice from under her big black hat, and we let her through. I walked out to the Strand and on to Waterloo Bridge, where I hung over the parapet for half an hour, waiting for the excitement to die down. Eventually I walked over the bridge and caught the tube home. I think Stan was with me.

Opera and opera singers have never had that effect since.

We heard a lot of concert music, too, the whole Beethoven symphony cycle, conducted by Victor de Sabata, at the Albert Hall. During this period a nice man in the office, overhearing me rave about some opera I had heard, tried to mentor me by inviting me to his home and playing music at me for four hours one bank holiday afternoon, while his wife fed us tea and cake. But he was something of a musicologist and I wasn't ready for his level of understanding—it was another twenty years before I discovered chamber music. My colleague had mistaken my enthusiasm for the easy passions of opera for a genuine ear which he wanted to educate. All afternoon he played his favourites at me, lecturing me on the intellectual subtleties of what I was hearing—at one point, I remember, he was explaining the quarter tones to be found in Arab music—while I tried to respond. But it was no use; I couldn't hear what he was talking about, and as the afternoon wore on it grew more and more difficult to manufacture a polite, *interested* response to each piece, until finally he released me, nearly paralysed with the effort I had been making, and I staggered off. Until that day, he had been glad to have a chat as I delivered his mail on my rounds, but he dropped me after that.

So once a week we saw and heard the best from the back of the gallery. We attended the theatre indiscriminately: Naunton Wayne in *Arsenic and Old Lace* or Paul Muni in *Death of a Salesman*—it was all grist to us. On Mondays we went to the pictures at the local cinemas, and on Saturdays we went to a dance hall in the doomed quest of a nice girl who went all the way. It sounds now like a very rich life, but it was only a rich seam, made possible because it was so cheap to do, and because we spent every penny we had on it, for the first three weeks of the month. Everything else was beyond me; we never visited a restaurant, not even for baked beans on toast, and it would have taken a year of not going out at night to save up the money for a spare suit.

In all this, Stan Yass was my constant companion and advisor. After we left school we formed a mutual exploration society, walking, learning to smoke, talking, trying to think. Only sex remained to be experienced and that was coming, Stan assured me, himself reassured by his elder brother. This brother had been a captain in the army and was now a chartered accountant, a very upwardly mobile type who had a lot of advice for Stan which Stan passed on to me, mostly about behaviour.

The proper word for Stanley and his brother is *aware*. They were conscious of what was going on around them whereas I lived unthinkingly until Stan pointed out what was happening. I knew nothing of his religion or culture for a year because there was no overt sign except that their food was better than I was used to, English but with a hint of garlic and a touch of pickled fish: tastier than ours. And then one Friday evening I called in to his house, noticed that the candles on their supper table were badly arranged and regrouped them as I had seen them arranged in the restaurants in Hollywood movies. No one said anything then, but later on, walking over the common, Stan explained the significance of the arrangement of candles in a Jewish house on a Friday night.

At the time it was no more or less interesting than if he had told me he was a Christian Scientist or a Quaker or Welsh. It was just something he reminded me of from time to time later on—when his mother wanted him to marry a nice Jewish girl, for example—to show me the difference between his family and mine.

The daytime poverty was made bearable by rationing, which excused any shabbiness in our clothes (but not the wearing of bookmakers' overcoats). Rationing had other benefits. My spinster aunt said that she never lived so well as she did during the war. Everybody had a job, Aunt Rose said, and the government made sure you had enough to eat. She regarded ration coupons not as limiting the quantity of food you could buy, but as guaranteeing that you would get something to eat, associating them with the only time of full employment she had ever enjoyed. She had been a chambermaid before the war at St. Ermine's Hotel in Victoria, often suddenly laid off in slack times and then having to choose between going in arrears on her rent, if her landlady let her, or going hungry. For her, it was worth being bombed occasionally to be sure of food and lodging. Peace, to her, meant being unsure you would have enough money for tomorrow's dinner, and when the war ended she left St. Ermine's and, on the advice of a pal of hers, took a job as an attendant in a public lavatory, where she found the work easier, the job permanent and pensionable, and the customers more agreeable.

Aunt Rose was a bit "slow," and may really have had the impression that ration coupons were a form of money. Certainly her limitations helped her to enjoy the happiest senility I have ever known of. She lived alone in a tiny basement in Stockwell. She visited us and my by-now-married sisters in rotation, every Tuesday afternoon for tea, so that if she failed to appear at the right house every six weeks or so, my brother Ron would check up on her. He generally looked in once a week anyway to make sure she had enough coals and kindling, and one night during a very fierce winter he found her unconscious, near death, suffering from hypothermia. She had become ill and unable to keep her fire in, and the cold added to her distress until she stayed in bed and nearly died. Ron got her to a hospital, and from there to a nursing home. When he next visited her, she no longer knew him, and she told him that now she was in heaven she was glad she had died; she had feared it before. Apparently when she woke up she was surrounded by figures in white, offering her cups of tea. This was so unusual for her that she assumed she was in paradise, and continued to believe that until she died, a year later. She left a very clear will, distributing all of her money among her nieces and nephews equally. We got forty-two pounds each. It was my first and last legacy, not an important sum, but not yet absolutely trivial, either, and I used it to buy a piece of costume jewellery for my wife in memory of my aunt.

Aunt Rose became a kind of political litmus test for me. After that, whenever I had doubts, I remembered that I should vote for the party that would guarantee the Aunt Roses of society enough to eat (without declaring a war) and a warm place to sleep, access to proper medical care without worrying about the cost, and at the end, a decent hospice when their wits are gone.

It wasn't only the Aunt Roses whose diets benefited from the war. The minister of food, I have read, was in 1938 preparing to use the coming war as an excuse to impose a better diet on the working class, by severely rationing tinned food, sugar, sweets and chocolate, butter and other fats, and by making it illegal to bleach the nutritional value out of bread. Everyone grew vegetables—DIG FOR VICTORY was the national slogan—and so, as well as good bread, even in winter, potatoes and the horrible Brussels sprouts were always available. Some things like orange juice were available only for children, and children were issued a third of a pint of milk twice a day at school. And if you went to a county school, you got a large hot dinner at noon, which not only supplemented the rations, but in many cases improved the diet. In 1940, after Dunkirk, a famous American war correspondent remarked on what poor physical specimens the British prisoners of war were, compared to their German captors. The war was won by a generation of soldiers who had grown up on white bread, fried meat, and tinned vegetables, followed (on Sundays) by tinned fruit. But the children of my generation were as fit as Hitler's youth as, finally, because of the war, we got enough to eat.

Fourteen

General Duties

AT MY LEVEL, the employees of the Asiatic Petroleum Company worked about two hours a day. We arrived at nine and discussed the previous evening's events, the radio plays we all listened to, what we had seen at the cinema, and how our personal and family lives had progressed since the day before. Gossip. The day's work was then laid out in the form of invoices to be calculated, letters to be drafted, endless checking of suppliers' invoices, collating them with the original quotations. (That is what I now think was happening. At the time I had no idea what the senior clerks were doing.) There was a coffee break at ten-thirty for about half an hour, then perhaps an hour of serious work until it was time to wash one's hands in preparation for "lunch," this new word for dinner in standard use in this society. The lunch hour was staggered so that the work of the department would not be brought to a halt, and so that the company dining room could handle everybody. You could leave at any time between 11:40 and 1:20 for an hour. In practice, a general hush fell on the office for two and a half hours. If you were not actually on your lunch hour, you did the crossword puzzle in your newspaper or you read the different newspapers the other clerks had brought. At three o'clock, there was a half-hour break for tea, and then once more an hour's work until four-thirty. The remainder of the afternoon, until five-thirty, was taken up with visits to the lavatory, more gossip, and trying to fill in the remaining crossword clues with the help of the other people who had bought the same paper (and, of course, done most of the crossword), little errands, and desk tidying. We worked one Saturday in three, and on these days we did not even pretend to do anything, just sat about in our sports jackets and grey flannel trousers, talking about the prospects for the weekend. Nowadays, when I hear or read of someone berating civil servants and suggesting a good dose of private enterprise would cure their laziness and inefficiency, I think of those days at the Asiatic Petroleum Company. The truth is that the company made so much money and paid us so little, relatively, that its inefficiency was hidden in its profits. The civil servants I see, on the other hand, like those in the Motor Vehicle Licensing Department, seem to work non-stop.

The outsiders among the office boys, the small group who saw that life had to have more to offer than the Asiatic Petroleum Company, waited and plotted, waited for something interesting to happen and plotted various escapes. Once, three of us decided to join the merchant navy, the modern version of running away to sea. We asked our parents first if that would be all right with them. Maurice's father told him to forget the idea. My mother broke down and cried, only the second time I had ever seen her in tears. (The first time was from the mixture of relief and anger when we found my father safe under the ceiling plaster after the bomb fell.) Now I learned that she had held on to herself for five years while three sons survived the evacuations of Dunkirk, Greece, and Crete (Joe), a lifeboat in the Barents Sea in January (Ron), and two years of being strafed while sweeping the North Sea for mines (Len). Now the fourth and last son wanted to leave, perhaps for good, without having the excuse of a war. I think she felt that finally she had failed. She had spent thirty-five years creating a family with no help or guidance from the previous generation, and little enough from my father, fiercely protecting the children and keeping her fingers crossed when the adults were in peril. And now when they were all safe again, one of them wanted to go. That is what she cried for, I think: the emotional bonds in our family were never discussed, and at seventeen I didn't know they existed. But I stayed ashore.

I had chosen the Asiatic Petroleum Company over the United Dairies, because its offices were in London, already, for me, a city of fable. I was reading at least two novels a week, most of them American, but also the big Victorian novels, especially Dickens, and the stories of Sherlock Holmes, and I was hungry to explore and experience the London I had read about. It began with the journey up to town. The simple way was to travel on the Underground from Colliers Wood to the bank, and this is what I did most of the time. But it is an ugly journey, being sucked down the tube at one end and vomited up at the other, trying to read a paper, standing up while holding on to a strap. Much more inconvenient, and taking a good twenty minutes longer, but infinitely more pleasant was the journey by Southern Railway, a proper train, with its suggestion of a real journey to somewhere. For this, I walked an extra fifteen minutes to Tooting Junction and caught the train either to London Bridge or to Blackfriars. If I went to London Bridge, I added the walk up Gracechurch street to my journey, but it was worth it for the walk across London Bridge. At that time, hardly anything had been rebuilt after the bombing and you could see for miles, St. Paul's in one direction, the monument straight ahead, and, of course, Tower Bridge downriver. And there were ships in the Pool of London then. If I went to Blackfriars station, I added the walk up Queen Victoria Street to the morning, a mile of almost entirely levelled buildings. I also added Hazel with whom at sixteen I was in love and who caught the same train at Mitcham Junction. Either way I enjoyed one more pleasure in the walk down Queen Victoria Street, or across London Bridge—my first cigarette of the day, which I disciplined myself to postpone until now. Whenever ex-smokers reminisce about their memories of their favourite cigarette, that morning Player's as I crossed London Bridge, inhaled over a near-virgin palate, is my own contribution. Looking back, I feel pretty sure that the pleasure of that first lungful was just as acute as the rush from the drugs I have managed to avoid.

Much was inconvenient, though, and when winter came I fell back permanently on to the Underground.

As well as Hazel, I was half in love with a laughing, blushing girl I'd met at work, a girl whose face is still vivid but whose name escapes me now—it ended in *a*, I think—Brenda?—but she lived in Mill Hill, as far north of the City as I lived south. With that kind of distance between us there was no point in pursuing her because of the problem of getting home at the end of the evening. Stan had got from his older brother the advice that a girlfriend should live between a three-ha'penny and a tuppeny-ha'penny bus ride away, that is, between one and two miles. Less than that and you would always be being seen with her by people you knew, including your family; more was too far to walk home. Stan's brother had developed a lot of rules like that.

I prowled around London in the lunch hours, too, with Maurice, office boy of the legal department, and my boon companion in the daytime. (He did his national service in the navy, and when he was demobilized he became a purser on the P. and O. lines, inviting me one night to dine with him on board when his ship was in dock, and that was the last time I saw him.) He and I could generally get outside the office for about an hour and a quarter during our lunch hour by slipping down to the dining room and gobbling our lunch on the company's time, and we travelled up to the Tower, and across to Lincoln's

Inn Fields, and once or twice down the East India Dock Road where W. W. Jacobs had set so many stories.

In the fullness of time, at eighteen, I joined the air force. Like my brother Len before me, I would have much preferred the navy, the only service that in peacetime more or less guaranteed an interesting national service in the ranks, radically different from clerking, but the air force was my second choice. You could apply for a commission in either the army or the air force but you had to sign up for three years, and if you failed the officers' training course, you were stuck with three years in the ranks. Very few people took the option. I chose the air force under the illusion that the standards for acceptance were slightly higher than for the army, that they were looking for a better class of recruit. Anybody could get into the army. This turned out not to be true. I also had the notion that air force recruits found nice girls easier to come by. This was true. Nice girls preferred airmen to soldiers, and I continued to try to persuade nice girls not to save it until they got married, with not much success. Meanwhile, it seemed to me, while I prowled the local towns wherever I was stationed, looking for goers who had passed their School Certificate, every hedge was alive with the sound of illiterate infantrymen shagging the local farm girls.

The next two years were as much of a waste of time as the previous two, or so it seemed then. After basic training we were given crude IQ tests as a result of which I was deemed suitable to be trained as a radar fitter. There were four levels of intelligence as measured by this test, from A to D, and four corresponding categories, and you had to take a trade within the category the IQ test placed you in. Category D, the one requiring minimal adaptability, consisted chiefly of the trades of RAF police and cook. I tested out as an "A," as did everyone else I knew, then and later, and requested training as a code clerk. But there was a surplus of code clerks left over from the war, so I was assigned to a sixty-week course as a radar fitter. I told them I had no mechanical ability of any kind, that I had failed general science at school, and, finally, that I did not have the slightest interest in radar or in fitting. All this was brushed aside by the officer in charge, a boy of my age with a Conservative party accent, who said that these things were decided at his level, not mine, and he didn't have time to argue.

I was sent to RAF Yatesbury where, within four weeks, I was failed out of the course. I did not fail deliberately. I just couldn't understand what they were talking about. Like many people, I have never understood what electricity is, and, like most people, I don't let that get in the way of my using the stuff, but for a long time, including my air force days, I believed that everyone understood something that was eluding me, and it stopped me from understanding the language of electricity, or even the vocabulary. (I have the same problem with double-entry bookkeeping. When an account is debited with a sum of money, I still have to ask, who is better off, the person the account is named for or us?)

I was hauled up in front of the officer in charge who called me a slacker, told me he didn't have time to argue, and that I was being reclassified for general duties (GD), roughly speaking, as a labourer, a member of the underclass, and that I was being posted to another station. Two days later I reported to the orderly room at RAF Netheravon, on the edge of the Salisbury Plain.

I was made to understand that by failing to qualify as a radar fitter, I had already wasted enough of the taxpayers' money, and by relegating me to general duties, the powers were punishing me by making sure that the rest of my two years would be a complete waste of time, for me and largely for them, too. In the event, it didn't work out like that. Some good came of it.

The GDs were the underclass, lower even than the cooks and the RAF police. We came under the general authority of the station warrant officer (SWO), a GD himself who had worked his way up the ladder until he was in charge of all the other GDs on the station, a kind of labour foreman. His equivalent in the army, the company or regimental sergeant major, was still a soldier by trade, trained to fight, but in the air force all the fighting is done by a few, and there is no equivalent to the infantry. GDs did all the dirty work, like sweeping roads, emptying privies, or earth closets, which were still common on air force stations off the route of the mains sewage—this sub-group were known as "turd-stranglers"—all the janitorial and non-specialized maintenance work. The SWO was the senior GD and therefore in charge of us, but in practice we rank and file were distributed around the station, each unit or office having one or two of us as servants to do whatever was beneath the skilled tradesmen. For a week or two I reported to the SWO's office every morning for a one-day task, like delivering coal, or cutting the CO's lawn. Then I worked in the post office for a week, where I was found one day by the acting education officer, a man who was in fact an ordinary aircraftsman like me, a wireless operator, I think, but with a university degree which had enabled him to persuade the authorities to let him run the vacant Education Office until a real officer was appointed. He had come in to the post office to get some help with a crossword puzzle from the erudite clerk who ran the office, and when I gave him the answer, he set about wangling me in to the Education Office as his assistant.

The SWO was furious. Like all his kind, he hated the idea of anyone slipping away from his authority, but there wasn't much he could do because my new boss was on good terms with the CO—I think he was courting the CO's daughter—and persuaded him to approve my transfer personally. Thereafter the SWO tried to frighten me by telling me it was only temporary. If he came across me by accident, he would stop, call me over close to him, and say, "Enjoy it while you can, lad-die. I'll 'ave you turd-strangling next week. Yus, or on the coal."

Once I was in the Education Office I had a good time. In 1947 the education branch of the air force was run by people like me and my boss, a patchwork of projects cobbled together at headquarters by old bomber pilots who were changing trades. The branch was hardly active during the war, in a cultural dimension, at any rate, and the activity now being generated was haphazard. We administered aptitude tests for per-sonnel about to be demobbed to help them discover any potential they might have been unaware of, and, periodically, a shortage would occur within the service of a particular trade, and an opportunity provided for personnel to reclassify into this trade. When this happened we processed the applications of anyone who wished to be retrained.

We were encouraged to make some gestures towards responding to the cultural needs of the men on the station, and we had a small fund for buying gramophone records to put on concerts in the can-teen, and for staging amateur dramatics. And we provided transporta-tion so that personnel could go into Salisbury to take evening classes, the truck returning after the pubs closed.

My own project was to search out the illiterates on the station and teach them their letters if they wanted. I enjoyed this: there is nothing so satisfying as imparting knowledge to a very bright, highly motivated blank slate, someone who has never been exposed to any kind of learn-ing whatsoever. My star was a Welsh shepherd boy who had been kept from school by his father who wanted him on the hills. For all he knew of the world, he might have been born in Sicily, until the air force and I saved him. I taught him to read and write in about three weeks. I got the same satisfaction twenty years later with the occasional "late bloomer," a sixties drop-out who suddenly in the seventies decided to drop back in. Such a student would gobble up what you had to offer faster than you could spoon it out.

On Saturdays a truck took us past Stonehenge into Salisbury where we spent the afternoon in the Salvation Army canteen. It was twenty years before I took a real look at Stonehenge, as a tourist. At the time, in 1947, a visit to those ancient stones would have meant valuable time lost when I could have been drinking tea and eating cream buns and playing ping-pong.

Afterwards, we came back in time to dance to "Bongo, Bongo Bongo, I don' wanna leave the Congo, oh, no, no, no, no, no!" at the Amesbury village dance. Here, one Saturday, I came as close to a fight, to being beaten up, as I had since junior school. There were never enough girls to go round near a military camp, and the Salisbury Plain is the base for tens of thousands of soldiers playing war games, because much of it is as barren as Thomas Hardy said. I got lucky one night, picked up a girl, and left the dance hall with her to walk her across the fields. Outside the hall, three soldiers were waiting.

"We're going to do you," one of them said.

Fear takes the form of rendering me immobile. I already had a small reputation for being brave because when bombs started to drop, I sat still, frozen to my seat, looking calm. Now I stood in the doorway, not moving. The girl grabbed my arm. "Come on," she said. "Never mind them."

"Why?" I said, finally, to the soldiers.

"You know fucking well why," the spokesman said.

"You took his girl," another said.

"Come on," the girl said. I shook her off. "I'll catch you up," I said to her. "Go on." She walked away.

"Come on, then," one of the soldiers said and clenched his fists. "You ain't going to get out of this one, mate."

"Yeah, come on," the other two said, and clenched theirs.

I didn't move.

"You knew she was his, didn't you?" the spokesman said.

"No," I said. "What's the difference? She's mine now."

The spokesman said, "You know we should kick your fucking teeth in, don't you?"

What I knew was that time was passing and they were becoming more and more human as it passed. They weren't three avengers: One of them had lost his girl and had asked his mates to back him up in claiming her back. The spokesman knew the proper drill in these matters, but none of them was very clear on procedure. If I had tried to run, they would have chased me, pushed me down, and kicked me in the head a couple of times, but I stayed where I was. Neither, though, did I confront them. But I knew my lines well enough, too. (All this I worked out later.) Besides, a small crowd had gathered, and all they could see was that three soldiers were about to beat up one airman. I said, "Try it. See what happens."

Eventually the third man spoke. "Gutless wonder," he said. "Brylcreem Boy," the spokesman said. The aggrieved soldier said, "Fucking try it next week, see what you get," and I knew it was all over. We waited for a few more minutes, then the third man said, "Come on. We'll miss the truck." He looked at me. "Fucking wanker's doom," he said. It had degenerated into name-calling. I said, "I'll bring a couple of mates next week, shall I?"

"Bring who you fucking like, tosser. Won't do you any good. We'll be waiting."

And then they left. No one had really wanted to fight, but honour had to be satisfied. I didn't bother to catch the girl up. If there was any truth in what the soldiers said, and there was, she shouldn't have come with me in the first place. At least she should have warned me. By the time I got back to camp I was feeling as hostile to her as I was towards the soldiers.

And then the orders came down for my posting to RAF Abingdon. My boss appealed to the CO, but the orders had come from Group

Headquarters, and the CO could do nothing. According to the records, Netheravon had more GDs than it was supposed to and Abingdon had fewer, and I got the short straw. The trains in those days were full of servicemen being shuffled around the country in ones or twos or threes, as someone in headquarters moved us about to make his numbers right. It was entirely arbitrary, at least at the GD level, who was sent.

So I left Netheravon, wondering what fate awaited me. If I had had a trade, like wireless operator, a posting to another station would merely be a nuisance. I would have been doing the same work in a different place, because it is an iron rule in the services that a tradesman cannot be asked to perform duties outside his trade, and all trades work must be performed by qualified tradesmen. In peacetime, that is. The whole thing was like a heavily unionized construction project. But a GD was, in the SWO's phrase, "Nothing, Fucking nothing," and nothing was beneath him.

It had been a pleasant interlude acting as an assistant education officer, but I was now once more facing the possibility of taking up turd-strangling.

Fifteen

A Spell of Education

ABINGDON WAS a nice little market town on the Thames, not far from Oxford. You could walk to the town from the station, and that summer was hot enough for us to spend most Sunday afternoons swimming in the river. Afterwards we ate poached duck eggs on toast and drank tea in the front room of a cottage, served by a woman who kept chickens and ducks, a tiny crack in the culinary gloom and a huge treat in the days when one small Polish, hard-boiled egg a week was the official ration. (All eggs in those days were Polish, for some reason, and all Polish eggs were tiny and smelled slightly of fish.)

On Saturdays, three or four of us visited Oxford for a walk round a college or two followed by an hour in Blackwell's and tea and buns at the Kardomah café. If the weather was fine, two or three of us pooled our money and rented a punt for an hour on the river. Most English novels about growing up that I had read included an Oxford scene, so I felt pretty much at home. Just before I was demobbed that autumn, one of my barrack mates who had finished his service and was now reading law at Queens College invited me for tea, which was the highlight of my Oxford experience. We weren't really pals, that law student and I; I think he was just doing a bit of social work, trying to create a vision for me of what was possible, what alternatives existed beside the Asiatic Petroleum Company. But first I had to cope with yet another SWO.

Upon joining or leaving a station, servicemen had to collect the signatures of everyone who might be interested in placing their names on record—the payroll office, obviously, but at least half a dozen others. The people who had to sign your arrival form were those whose interest lay in knowing who the new arrivals were. The departure form was mostly signed by the people you might owe goods to. One of the people most interested in my arrival was the SWO who had to sign my form twice, once as the allocator of a bed in a barrack room, and the second time as the senior NCO in charge of GDs. This SWO's eyes lit up as he took down my name and rank. "GD," he said. "GD, eh? Report to me tomorrow morning after parade. Got a nice job for you."

Coal or roads? I wondered. I was probably spared the honey wagon. I had seen no outside toilets so far. But one of the signatures I had not yet got was that of the education officer. The point of getting his signature was to give him a chance to meet newly arrived personnel and acquaint them with the services he had to offer. When I presented my form for his signature, he said, "Welcome to Abingdon, Wright. I won't hold you up now, but you must come back and see us. Perhaps I can help you. Did you know that you can take your School Certificate by correspondence now? It's a long road, of course, but you could make a start."

He had medal ribbons from the war, and a pilot's wings over his pocket; a former aircrew who had decided to make a career of the peacetime force. Perhaps he, too, had once been a clerk in the Asiatic Petroleum Company and preferred to keep the rank he had achieved in the war, even, more commonly, come down a rank or two rather than go back to Bishopsgate. Stories of wing commanders returning to their old jobs as school janitors were legion then. This man also had a pipe and a bushy moustache and was trying to be chummy. I had already taken in the fact that he was alone in the office and needed a clerk.

"I have my School Certificate, sir," I said, trying to indicate by my tone that I was not bragging but just trying to show that I might be useful to him.

"Do you, indeed? And what were you doing at your last station? Who was the education officer there?"

"We didn't actually have anyone in your position, sir. I shared the duties with another chap."

He took out his pipe. "In what way?"

I rattled off the list of tasks I had performed, quoting the numbers of the official forms we used in the Education branch to make it clear I wasn't bullshitting him; I showed my familiarity with the latest orders from Group Headquarters, and I ended with a little anecdote about how I taught my Welsh shepherd.

"Really?" he said. "Really? And what have you been assigned here?"

"Nothing yet, sir. The SWO decides that. I have to report to him tomorrow morning."

"Really?" he said again. "Hang on a mo'." He picked up the phone and asked to be connected to the station adjutant. "George," he said, or Hector or Percy. "Paul here. That little matter we were talking about. I think I have a solution. You can keep your clerk. There's a GD in my office now just arrived on the station from Netheravon, where he worked in the Education Office. He says he ran the place. No, I don't think he's pulling my pisser, no." He winked at me. "Yes. I want him. All right. Will you arrange it with the SWO? Here's his name and number. Right. Thanks, George." He put the phone down and turned back to me. "You don't mind being downgraded from acting education officer to dogsbody, do you? Good. So finish up this form and come back here."

"What about the SWO, sir?"

"What about him?"

"He's the one in charge of GDs, sir. He's the one who says what I do."

"The man I talked to was the station adjutant. *He's* the one who tells SWOs what to do. All right? Off you go, then, and come back and tell me how to run this place."

Later I learned he meant just that. He had only arrived himself three days before, reassigned from other duties. He was much less qualified than I was. His School Certificate was on a par with mine, but he didn't have my experience. He badly needed guidance.

The SWO was furious. He had not yet put the second signature on my form, and when I reappeared in his office to tell him I had already been assigned to the Education Office, he said, "All right, laddie. But don't get your feet under the table. I'll have you out of there in two days. Then we'll give you a try in the tin room."

I knew about the tin room, a place of heat and steam and grease underneath the kitchen where the huge tins the food was baked in were cleaned. As they were used, these tins were thrown through a hole in the kitchen floor and collected by the creatures below, usually minor criminals who had been caught with a button undone. But if the guard-room could not provide enough minor offenders, then the SWO sent in some GDs. I had done the job in my early days at Netheravon, a stint that coincided with my introduction to Dostoyevski. Afterwards, the two experiences always stayed together in my mind.

I returned to the education officer and told him, with as blank a face as I could manage, what the SWO planned for me. "Don't worry about him, old boy," he said, and picked up the phone. "Get me the station adjutant, would you?" he asked.

The education officer and the SWO struggled over me for about a week, the SWO continually circling the office like a hungry predator, trying to find a way to pick me off. But my new boss prevailed. Thereafter, and until I found the way to thwart him permanently, the SWO watched me, like SWOs everywhere, crooning, whenever I came into range, "I'll 'ave you yet, laddie." The closest he came, late in the summer, was to get the administration officer, the chief clerk, to agree that the Education Office should have a proper clerk, a tradesman, who would free me to do work for which he desperately needed me, like shovelling coal. It happened that the administration officer had a surplus of clerks, so he agreed, but a pal of mine in the SWO's office had tipped us off about the plot, and the education officer had already put into motion an emergency scheme we had prepared, purely for my benefit. He sent me on a two-week course, designed, by teaching me typing and familiarity with some simple forms, to upgrade me from GD to clerk. "Clerk" was a trade, so two weeks later I came back a tradesman, having done so well in the course that I was reclassified as clerk, first class, the height of my career in the air force. The real point was that the SWO could no longer touch me. His only hope was if I committed some offence—he was responsible for assigning punishments to minor criminals—but I never gave him a chance. And to give him his due, it would have been easy enough to frame me ("Failing to salute an officer," for example) but he never did. I think he might have been just having fun, teasing me, or perhaps because with my School Certificate and my Mitcham County School accent, I wasn't a typical GD, so he'd picked me out as someone who needed to get his hands dirty. Even if he was just teasing me, it felt like a reign of terror, as teasing usually does.

Somewhere about now, in 1948 or 1949, the government became aware that the war was over, and yet they were still recruiting every eighteen-year-old for combat. There were skirmishes being fought in the East, but not by RAF Transport Command. I have no idea how many men were stationed at RAF Abingdon, several hundred, anyway, but we sometimes didn't have any aircraft. Occasionally a plane from another base would land on a training flight, and very senior officers were ferried around, but our own hangars were usually empty. And although three-quarters of the men were employed servicing each other, we had no core from which work could flow, no planes, no missions, no training responsibilities. We used to kid the aircraft mechanics, suggesting they get a dummy plane to practise on; they were already reduced to stripping down and reassembling the engines of old plane carcasses that had been shot down in the war.

Inevitably this kind of make-work activity created a widespread desire among the recruits to get this nonsense done with so that life could begin again. We had nothing but contempt for the "regulars," those who had signed up to make the air force their life. They seemed deficient in some hard-to-name area, not intelligence, but will, or perhaps imagination. Perhaps even hope. It seemed unthinkable to the rest of us to abandon the possibility of a golden future, to limit oneself to a future in which every quantity was already known, and the only measure of happiness was the slow increase of physical comfort, free from worry; safety, in fact. It seemed less than human, an extension, in uniform, of the Asiatic Petroleum Company.

Thus there occurred an increasing awareness on the part of the government that they should do something about preparing us for the outside world, to employ our time usefully. The flaw in this thinking was that if it were taken to its conclusion, then training for civilian life would begin the day the men were recruited, because there was little enough to train them for in the service. The main result for me was that there occurred a rapid expansion of the education branch, charged now with providing interesting diversion on a day-to-day basis, and with giving the men access to some real education and retraining that would help them later. It suddenly became possible for conscripts to study a wide range of subjects by correspondence, and to enrol in local colleges and technical schools, in civilian courses and programs. Very few took advantage of these new opportunities, but the Education Office had to grow simply to advertise them, to make the men aware of what they might do. Soon, in addition to our education officer, we had an assistant education officer, Pilot Officer P., not a former rear-gunner but one of a new breed of education officer, specially recruited and trained for the job.

Pilot Officer P., an Oxford graduate, was the first religious person I had ever come close to. I was raised an embarrassed Anglican, but it was so clearly *their* religion, not ours, that, like everybody else I knew, I ignored it. But Pilot Officer P. was not a man to be ignored. He was learned, courteous, modest, and he planned to be an Anglo-Catholic priest. Of him I made my first semi-literate but serious inquiries about the absurdity, even the indecency, after the spiritual squalor in which Germany had drowned Europe, of believing in an old man with a white beard up in the sky.

Pilot Officer P. did me the courtesy of providing me with much better questions for my case, and then responded to them. He never moved me from my position, but he did convince me of his sincerity, and stopped me from assuming that the clergy were all frauds. I had long before worked out with Stan that since no thinking person could possibly believe in virgin births and tricks with loaves and fishes and all the rest of it, or understand why God, or at least the Vatican, hadn't done something about the Holocaust, then the intelligent clergy must be using the job as a cover to perform charitable work. But Pilot Officer P. was a Christian, and as a Christian he didn't demolish my intellectual fumblings, but clarified them, letting me grow up in them, as it were. He introduced me to the simple understanding that doubt does not destroy faith, but that faith requires doubt in order to exist.

He was also interested in my politics, again leading me into a clearer understanding of my position, and providing me with a defence of it.

I was a socialist by instinct, reinforced by the fact that the Young Conservatives in Mitcham were such twits, but also by a conviction that while the Labour cabinet wanted to improve my lot, the Conservatives wanted to improve their own. Pilot Officer P. lent me a book by Bernard Shaw, a guide to socialism, judging that it was pitched at a good level for me then. He was right. Shaw was the first non-fiction writer I read who was as interesting as the novelists I was consuming. Orwell was the next, specifically his *Down and Out in London and Paris*. Nothing has ever had the effect on me that those two had. Then after I had read Shaw's book, Pilot Officer P. explained to me what *conservative* really meant for him, and why he was one. I understood him then, and because of my admiration for him I should like to have become one, but it was no use. I was stuck with the Labour party. I have only met one true conservative since, in the sense that Pilot Officer P. used the word, someone who is dedicated to preserving the best of the past and the present to take into the future and who accepts responsibility for the community's welfare—for the poor. I've now given up hope of finding in politics enough conservatives in this sense to fill a telephone booth.

As well as Pilot Officer P., we had Sergeant X, a small, upright, amused Yorkshireman, a graduate of Cambridge, who planned to be a teacher of young children. He also bothered with me. There was a growing despair within me as the future approached, and out of this despair came a need to find another future. What Pilot Officer P. and Sergeant X did was encourage me to dream, by taking me seriously, helping me to look within and without to see what I could find. They performed very much the service that a decent schoolmaster like Mr. Thomas might have done, three years before. But they did it lightly. They both agreed that I should see if there was anything available for me other than the Asiatic Petroleum Company, but neither was irresponsible with his advice, knowing that choices that had been available to them were not necessarily open to me. Mostly I was left with a sense that I was privileged to be among such a civilized group, where rank was irrelevant. Over the years I have steadily grown more grateful to those two men. When my time was up, Pilot Office P. gave a little dinner for me in the Taj Mahal, in Oxford. It was my first authentic Indian meal, but more important it was my first dinner out, the first serious meal in a restaurant, let alone the first time I had been a guest of honour.

All the while, I was reading. Hemingway was the favourite—I still have a notebook from about that time which contains embarrassing imitations of his sentences—but I also ate up Steinbeck, Dreiser, Sinclair Lewis, and Balzac. Big and meaty was what I seemed to want then, and there was very little to satisfy such an appetite in English fiction between the wars. Hugh Walpole (whom we studied for School Certificate)? Galsworthy? Gentlewomen's literature; there was nothing for me there. Some people in those days were still reading Warwick Deeping, but in me such writing performed the service of fomenting the beginnings of a critical faculty, as I realized that it was me that Sorrell hated and feared. Perhaps I experienced the first stirrings of what later became a powerful critical fashion, because I learned that a book's meaning depended on the class of the writer and of the reader, that as soon as I associated myself with the servants in the novels, whole new patterns of meaning started to emerge, different indeed from what the writer believed to be his own objective understanding of what he was saying. And I began to have the courage to find ridiculous the attempts by some of the major writers to portray anyone not of their class, and to see it as a sign that they were, in the end, second-class themselves. Good intentions weren't enough: Forster's Leonard Bast, for example, was absurd, a creature constructed out of an attempt to shift a bohemian lifestyle down the social scale to where it would never have been tolerated, all for the sake of creating a plot.

There was one book which all my cronies, at home or in the air force, revered, Jerome K. Jerome's *Three Men in a Boat*, unreadable now, but for a long time the funniest book I had ever read. In August of that summer, Stan, whose national service was deferred until he was qualified as a surveyor, suggested we follow in Jerome's wake, and row from Kingston to Oxford, through Abingdon, and back over two weeks.

Three Men in a Boat is a dangerous book if read at the wrong age. The story of how three men ("to say nothing of the dog") rowed up the Thames from Kingston to Oxford and most of the way back generates enormous affection in its readers because it is very funny; but also because it seems to describe a kind of paradise that the young reader may try to inhabit.

Stan and I rented a camping skiff at Kingston and rowed up to Abingdon and back, avoiding Oxford but otherwise carefully duplicating the adventure in a misplaced act of homage. We wanted to share in the world of Jerome K. Jerome, and we thought we could do it by spending two weeks on the Thames.

We observed all the rituals, including rereading the packing scene and doing our own packing the night before. Organizing food was a lot easier for us than it was for Jerome because rationing was still severe, but we had saved up enough tins of Spam and packets of cornflakes and powdered milk to last, and from somewhere Stan had got hold of two jars of peanut butter (a new treat for me).

The weather was perfect. Once it got so warm that we tried to tow the boat while swimming. We navigated up to Abingdon, noting the text's accuracies—the waterfront at Reading was still ugly—and the changes that had taken place since Jerome's time. Physically the banks of the river had not changed much since late Victorian times; two world wars and a depression had restricted the inventions of the twentieth century to those who could afford them, and there were not enough power launches to bother us. However, in 1949, the references to the meals Jerome ate might have come from Samuel Johnson's England as far as we knew—we had never seen a porterhouse steak, or heard of a cottager who had five pounds of bacon handy to serve to three hungry young men.

But the rest was as Jerome described it. All through that first week we rowed and towed ourselves upriver, and on the Sunday we started back. The weather stayed glorious. Then, on Thursday afternoon, I went through precisely the experience they did, although it was years before I realized it. Readers will remember that in the book it had been raining for days on the return journey, and at first the three men accepted this as part of the experience of nature, "the river in all its moods." Gradually the rain soaked through their bedding, their food, and themselves, and they became good and sick of it, and abandoned their boat and slunk back up to London for a dinner with fresh crisp loaves of French bread and bottles of burgundy, and went on to visit the music hall.

In our case, the sun continued to blaze down; but while we were eating lunch at Henley I had a revelation: I discovered that I was a cockney and bored stiff with nature. I badly needed an injection of urban entertainment. That afternoon, making excuses to Stan, who was a purist, I walked into the town and found a cinema to watch *Gaslight* and eat a choc ice. I emerged into the daylight as embarrassed and content as a marriage counsellor who has spent the afternoon in a bordello. Stan was waiting for me, glum and resigned—I was always disappointing him—and we rowed on to Kingston. I kept up a stream of bright chat about the terrific holiday, but I had let down the expedition and he couldn't forgive me.

But I know now I was more attuned to Jerome than Stan was. As I read it now, the rain in the book is just a literary device. They had had ten days of cold meat, cake, and bread and jam, and nature, and each other, and Jerome invented the rain to cover the fact that they were at the end of their patience. Like me, they were townies, and they had mistaken the pleasures of dabbling in nature, on a punt on Sunday afternoon, for the real thing.

Jerome couldn't admit this, of course. Like many comedians, he got soppy when he tried to be serious, and as a late Victorian he had inherited that religiosity of feeling about the natural world that Romanticism had turned into. This pious reverence for nature filters through the book like a miasma; it infects the story and our response to it, especially during adolescence. All those awful passages we now skip, about the river's beauty at dusk or dawn, obligatory mumblings from a conventional Victorian sentimentalist, nevertheless leave an impression on a young mind that Eden can be achieved by hiring a boat and rowing up the river for two weeks. A funny Eden. Of course it can't.

The only way to survive two weeks in a boat, alone or with friends, is to take plenty of books, including *Three Men in a Boat*, and find out what's playing in the cinemas along the shore.

Sixteen

The Last of England

AND THEN, in October, my intake was demobilized and I took the train up to Blackpool, handed in my uniform, accepted the free civilian "demob" suit, which I thought my father could wear in his stables, and took the train to Colliers Wood, still wondering, as I had been for months, what I was going to do next. There was no immediate problem about finding work: the law required your last employer to take you back after national service, so I was returning to the Asiatic Petroleum Company, now called Shell, to work as an administration trainee. But that would be as temporary as I could make it. For the last four years I had been marking time, generally waiting. The decision to break away from the pattern laid out for me, a "good job" (i.e., a steady job that required School Certificate, with a pension at the end), marriage begun in two rooms in Balham, and so on, was not to be undertaken lightly, except by that rare individual who knows exactly what he wants to do from the age of ten or so and simply ignores any advice or attempt to divert him. I think this is common among actors and painters, but I had no such positive conviction, only the very strong negative one that I didn't want to look forward to much more of what I was doing.

In Colliers Wood, despite the war, the forces against change were very strong. We were only ten years out of a depression in which we had not actually gone hungry but my father had once had to line up at the equivalent of a food bank to take care of the groceries. And my parents had grown up in the class that had always lived hand to mouth, one week at a time. The kind of regular employment such as my father eventually achieved put them in a slightly different category, thus my mother's whole efforts for us were directed towards maintaining our position in society by slotting us into regular employment of any kind. In my parents' eyes, my superior education had put me in a position of respectability and security undreamt of by them at my age. So what was wrong?

They never understood, when I told them, why I had to leave the Asiatic Petroleum Company, but they did accept that I had to. That tiny bit of extra education had put a gap between us, not intellectually but socially, just as our neighbour had feared, so that I was a stranger to them by the time I was thirteen and at twenty was no more than a boarder in my own house. But I do not think I would have had the energy to break away without the perspectives I acquired through the years I had spent, first, at the Asiatic Petroleum Company and then in the air force. Those "wasted" four years made me see my situation more clearly, made me know my priorities, even if I could not verbalize them, and thus may have allowed me to avoid a life of quiet desperation.

At first an acute shortage of office space in London after the war caused the company to locate some of its offices in the Lensbury Club, the sports-and-leisure facility built for the employees on the bank of the Thames at Teddington. There I went to join a sort of general department where, the theory was, trainees would get an overview of how the company worked before they were assigned to a real department to purchase supplies or sell oil. I think that was the idea. I never found out. I was assigned a desk, one of a group of four, in a large room of about a dozen such groups of desks. Here we played pencil-and-paper games and once more did the *Times* crossword for about a third of the day, washed our hands and ate and (in my case) studied the *Racing Form* which was beginning to interest me in a pauperish way for another third, and worked in a fashion for the other third. The work must have been utterly trivial because the only memory I have is of adding up a few columns of figures, checking the work of someone else, but what the figures referred to I have forgotten, if I ever knew. It was not a memorable time. Most of all I started to plan again, started to plot my escape. The spell that the idea of security can cast over a timid youth once he joins a pension plan was broken.

Returning like this, spending the days killing time and the evenings reading about other worlds, I knew that this must stop. I had been here before, but in the interim I had met Pilot Officer P. and Sergeant X, and had tea in an Oxford college, and had talked about writing long into the evening with Tom Brennand, a journalist and barrack-room mate, and I had been encouraged to feed my discontent and to respond to it. What I had to do was figure out a way to create that response. Money was still very, very scarce and I saw no point in leaving the Asiatic Petroleum Company to join United Dairies. But when the department moved up to London, to Houndsditch Warehouse, near Petticoat Lane, I found the days were as unfulfilling as ever, and now the London nights had lost some of their magic. It had been great at sixteen to sit in theatre galleries, then walk the streets with Stan, broke, talking about what we'd seen, but now, at twenty, I wanted to participate. Sex was the main item on the agenda (although, as Philip Larkin said, sexual intercourse had not really been invented yet), sex and writing and travel.

I think sociologists must by now have identified the decade from the end of the war to the arrival of the Beatles as the end of the

Victorian Age, an age whose stated values had gradually shifted down the social scale until they arrived at the lower middle classes. Above us, the children of the middle classes were beginning to break free, and below us the conventions had never held such strong sway. But for us, made genteel by the grammar school, it was still hard to pick up suitable girls, nice girls who would take their clothes off. The youth clubs catered to horny-handed artisans, and the only alternative was the still unthinkable Young Conservative Club. And then, when you found a girl, there was the elaborate dance of who pays. In spite of the fact that girls who could type at this time were in demand and earned much more than male clerks, protocol demanded that if you asked a girl out, you spent two weeks' pocket money on her—on cinema seats, on chocolates, and on bus fares. It was ruinous. If a second date seemed worthwhile, protocol said that she should show her worth by offering to pay, but you still had to refuse. She did pay the third time, by slipping a ten-shilling note into your hand in the cinema queue, but by this time you were nearly bankrupt. All this was for half an hour's groping in her doorway.

You couldn't carry on like this, and once you both decided that you wanted to continue, you would eventually get engaged and start saving up, thus openly sharing the money problem and making canoodling easier. People who got engaged sometimes did it. At least they discussed, endlessly, whether to do it or not. Usually couples decided not to do it until their wedding night. Contraceptive devices were illegal—you bought French letters at the barber's—and without leisure, adequate lighting, and privacy, they could be embarrassing to use. Still, just discussing the problem at least would lead to some more serious interlocking, of a kind unavailable to the casual date. Where to do it was still a problem. There were no cars to provide back seats; engaged couples had to wait for one set of parents to take a night out, or go down to the seaside for a night in a boarding house if parents could be persuaded to believe that it was a harmless excursion involving six or eight members of the bicycle club. Otherwise it was Wimbledon Common.

Why didn't more of the couples simply get married? What were they saving for? First, the money to get into a flat. No new housing had been built since 1939, except for some prefabricated houses, intended for the temporary alleviation of what had become an enormous shortage. Couples who before the war might have expected to start life in a little bungalow with all mod cons now thought they were lucky if they found two rooms with a gas ring and a shared bathroom. Rents for existing accommodation were controlled, but the landlord could insist you paid a ransom for the "fixtures," no more perhaps than a pair of ragged curtains but enough to meet the legal demand. It amounted to a kind of key money, to be paid up front before the flat could be rented. So it became a common pattern for a young couple to be engaged for two celibate years before they had saved enough for the key money and the minimum furniture. They abjured costly entertainments and holidays, consoling themselves with day trips by coach to the seaside and long walks in the country with some very heavy petting. Sometimes they gave up cigarettes, even newspapers. All this to live in semi-poverty in a basement in Croydon. Because (the other convention of the time) after they were married, she stayed home and they had to live on his wages. And inevitably, given the state of all the arts, she soon became pregnant.

Within a few years, all this would change, but we didn't know that.

There simply had to be an alternative. If this was the responsible way, then the alternative was irresponsibility. About now I began to ponder all the pleasant news I had heard of another world I had glimpsed at my sister's wedding, five years before, to which she had invited three Canadians she worked with at her air force station, two men and a girl, people so agreeable that I wondered if they came from a better world than mine. The experience of meeting those three had been augmented since by meeting a nice girl from Manitoba—and confirmed by a man from Calgary who worked for Shell for a time. I decided to emigrate to where these people came from.

Not a lot was known about Canada in my circle. The Canadian Pacific Railway took seven days to cross the country, and if you took the train, you would see a landscape of rock, trees, wheat, the Rocky Mountains, ice, and snow. The country was policed, benevolently, efficiently, and in dedicated fashion, by chaps in red coats called the Royal North-West Mounted Police who were mainly the younger sons of English earls. Most Canadians were farmers, or loggers, or trappers, but there were some folk living in cities (there was one city in each province), strung across the country. A BBC favourite radio show in Britain in the late forties was the "Big Bill Campbell Show," which aired on Sunday morning and featured a band of English cowpokes celebrating the spirit of Canada in song and story. The signature tune of the show was "Springtime in the Rockies," which they sang around the campfire in the BBC studios as they ate flapjacks covered in maple syrup.

All Canadians smoked Sweet Caporals and played hockey, except the Indians, who played lacrosse. Everyone owned a large car and Canadian boys routinely drove a hundred miles in an evening on a date. The people in a province called Quebec all spoke French, but everyone else spoke English, and would be pleased to welcome any Englishmen who wanted to live there.

This was our image of Canada, assembled from *Rose Marie*, from children's stories about derring-do along the fur-trading routes (in which all the villains were half-breeds, called Frenchie) and uninformed by Canadian literature, which apparently didn't exist.

Canada, we knew, used to be part of the Empire, and was now a member of the Commonwealth, but geographically it was joined to

America. Like most of my friends I was soaked in American literature and Hollywood movies, and I wanted to see America, the land where it all came from, but the idea of being alone and broke in the U.S. was daunting—the images of poverty in Steinbeck were vivid. But no such image of Canada existed. Canada sounded like a place where I would never be a foreigner, where the relationship with the mother country would guarantee that I would be regarded, if in dire straits, as a relative, whereas in the United States I might become a hobo, whatever that meant. By emigrating to Canada, I could partake of the American dream without much risk.

So I thought, and so it proved to be.

The word *emigrant* conjured up an association of clearing the land and building a cabin, of starting life again. The log-cabin days were over, but the notion that this was a major journey, not easily or soon retraced, remained. To start with, in 1951 you went by ship. I have an old etching of a group of people—a family of husband, wife, children, and a Magwitch-like grandfather, all sitting on a bench on the dockside. It is entitled *The Emigrants' Last Look at England*. The idea that emigration was for life survived into the fifties, until cheap air travel and decent wages began to shuttle everyone back and forth at whim.

The cheapest passage on a ship cost fifty pounds, or two hundred and fifty dollars. I wanted to avoid Toronto or Vancouver because every other English emigrant seemed to be heading to one or other of these two cities. It was my very sound instinct that the only way I was going to experience this new world for myself was by avoiding the English and the Scots, not by sitting around drinking Watney's Ale, if I could find it, reading old copies of the *News of the World*. As well, the only people I knew in Canada lived in Manitoba, so I headed for Winnipeg. This meant I needed the money for the train fare and, finally, enough to live on for a month, by which time I would have a job or perish.

(I wouldn't let any child of mine set off so lightly clad today, but it seemed a fair provision for the adventure, a long way up from the tin of treacle biscuits and the piece of cheese Laurie Lee set out with. He wasn't crossing an ocean, of course, but then, I didn't have a violin.)

This was my budget; the problem was how to get hold of even this modest sum. I think I made up my mind to go in the spring of 1950, and the first passage I could get was on the Greek Line, sailing in June of 1951. A year was about what I needed.

I had a tiny gratuity from the air force, and by resigning from the Asiatic Petroleum Company I got back my pension contributions, perhaps fifty pounds, enough for the boat fare, and the rest I would have to save. I went to work in an electrical-parts factory on the Kingston bypass, a job which let me work overtime, and I started to put in twelve-hour days, earning twice what I did before.

I saved hard for a year, just like an engaged couple, managing to put away about two pounds a week. Soon I realized I needed some clothes for the trip, especially a raincoat and some shoes. I cut down to five cigarettes a day and bought an old bicycle to save on fares to the factory. Then, on Saturdays, I went to work for my brother Ron.

Ron had had trouble working for anyone else when he came out of the merchant navy. Once he worked briefly as a packer in a glass factory. A problem cropped up with a very delicate little vase which had been shipped three times and arrived broken each time. "Can't anyone find a way to pack this thing safely?" the factory owner asked. "I'll do it," Ron said. "Out the back, and don't watch me." Three hours later Ron reappeared. "Done," he said.

Everyone trooped out to see what he meant. They found a six-foot-square crate that Ron had spent most of the afternoon building, filled with straw and shredded paper. In the middle of the packing, like a pea under a mattress, he had put the tiny vase. Everyone, including the foreman, roared with laughter at the ludicrousness of Ron's solution.

Everyone except the factory owner, who said, "Finally, someone with some brains. How much do we pay you?" Ron said, "Not enough to work for this arsehole," pointing at the foreman, and asked for his cards, the documents you carried from one employer to another.

"What they should have done," he said afterwards, "was give me the vase and sent me in a taxi to deliver it by hand. That would have been the cheapest. It was only going five miles away. But when I suggested it, they all thought that I was looking for a skive, and they broke another vase trying to find a better answer. I was sick of them."

Inevitably he went to work for himself, erecting wooden fences on new-housing estates, and he got plenty of work because he could build a fence faster and more cheaply that the main contractor could with his own men. He did it by working like a galley slave. I lasted three Saturdays, and I've never worked so hard before or since, even when laying twelve-inch pipe in a trench in northern Alberta. You dig a hole, hammer in a post, put in the stringers from post to post, and nail on the planking. Non-stop. On the run. In the rain. On the third Saturday I was finished by mid-afternoon. It was sleeting, and by two o'clock I couldn't go on. Ron gave me a day's wages and let me go. I worked at the factory for another two months, and then it was time to embark.

Joe gave me an old leather suitcase he had bought second-hand twenty years before, when he was a travelling salesman with Crosse and Blackwell, and my brothers and sisters passed the hat round and came up with five pounds. Two nights before I sailed, I spent too much money taking Marion up to the West End to see *Venus Observed* with Laurence Olivier. Afterwards we went to a Lyons Corner House and had a glass of Cointreau, a first for both of us. There was only friendliness between us now. I had picked her up (or she had picked me up) at a dance in the local art school two years before and we began a relationship which flared briefly without consuming us, then flickered low without actually dying out as we stayed in touch while others came and went, and it seemed right that we should spend a last evening together. For a year I had been too engrossed in saving my boat fare to hunt seriously for her replacement, contenting myself with clutching one or two girls from the office. But no one claimed my full attention, and since they were beginning to look for husbands they saw me as just as temporary as I saw them.

It was a wistful evening. The play was not engrossing enough to take my mind off the coming journey, and though there were no illusions between us, the very form of the evening—boy/girl/parting/perhaps for ever—created its own melancholy. The flame guttered briefly over the Cointreau, but it went out quietly enough in a friendly kiss on her doorstep.

My father said cheerio the evening before and went off to his stable, and my mother, who still didn't understand why I was going, went to bed early with a headache. Two friends called round and we went off to a pub for a farewell drink and when I got home my mother called through the bedroom door that Len had stayed home at her suggestion in case I wanted to go out and have a drink with him. It hadn't crossed my mind, because we now lived in different worlds, and my mother should have told me *before* I went out with my pals, but it was too late now and I went to sleep feeling lousy. Len was already asleep. In the morning I woke Len up to say I was sorry I didn't realize he had stayed home for me, but he said that was all right and turned over and went back to sleep.

The next morning she called goodbye through the bedroom door and Joe came with me to see me on the boat train at Waterloo station, saying solemnly, as we parted, "If you're not home by September, I won't expect you until next year," wanting to let me know that he was aware of the size of the step I was taking. I next saw him nine years later. I never saw my parents again.

Seventeen

The Emigrant

THE SS *CANBERRA* was old in 1951. (I have seen the name since, obviously referring to another ship, and I've often wondered what governs the naming of ships. Can you simply decide to call your ship the *Normandie*, now that the original has been broken up? Or the *Queen Mary*?)

Our *Canberra* was small and slow; I think it had been converted into a troopship in the war and the new owners had borrowed from its experience to see just how many people they could cram on to it. I shared a cabin with three other people, a wedge-shaped space with four bunks that overlapped at the pointed end of the cabin. Only one person could dress at a time, and we washed communally in a bathroom along the corridor. We ate in several long rows in a dining room like an army mess hall. For entertainment, we played simple board games, listened to a German piano trio play "Eine Kleine Nachtmusik" and selections from Romberg and the Strausses. I suspect they were good musicians, but their customers wanted music to dance to or to sing along with. Once a day the German waiters lined up and sang a drinking song, usually the one that begins, "Ein, zwei, drei . . ."

There were two bars, a large noisy one in the middle of the ship and a tiny quiet one at the back that eventually became the bar of choice for the Anglo-Saxons. There seemed to be only a handful of single English people on board; the journey we were embarked on was not a vacation cruise and most of the passengers were off to start a new life. They were too apprehensive about the future to enjoy the present very much, as they sat together in tight little groups, watching their money.

The ship had begun its journey in the Baltic, at Bremerhaven, and was half-full when it reached Southampton. Many of the passengers had been refugees, including some officially designated displaced persons. There was a Ukrainian pair, a mother with her grown-up daughter whom the mother guarded with a fierceness that spoke of rough experiences in the recent past. In my ignorance, I wondered how they would manage in Winnipeg where I was sure everyone spoke English or French. There were Lithuanians, Estonians, and Latvians who had managed to slip away from the Russians. There was a poor Dane—"I'm just a poor Dane," he said to everyone, by way of making himself welcome. There was an Irish boy who spent the whole trip leaning over the rail in the front of the ship, looking for land and worrying. If you went near him, he had a question for you. "Do you think we'll have to buy a fur coat for the winter?" he would ask in genuinely worried tones. "Would an ordinary one do with a couple of pullovers?" Or, "I hear you can't get a dascent cup o' tea in Montreal. Is that right, do you think?" Or, "They say they won't let you into a hospital if you haven't got any money. What do they do with you if you get into an accident?" But these were not real questions, just the external signs of the worry track unrolling in his head. If you tried to respond, he never listened.

There was a Norwegian boy with white hair and a sky-blue tracksuit who never said anything and spent the nights in a sleeping bag on deck. If it rained, he laid out his bag under a lifeboat. No one got a word out of him, and we wondered if he was a deaf-mute.

There was a large group of Scots, including a gang from the Gorbals, and a boy who sang "The Skye Boat Song" with a hand beside his mouth like a street-singer while his tiny fierce mother kept us quiet by glaring round the room, daring anyone to speak. And there was a small group of Germans, one of whom had to be persuaded on the final night that it would not be tactful to wear the uniform of a Luftwaffe officer at the fancy-dress dance. The boys from the Gorbals were offended just by finding themselves on a ship with Germans so soon after the war and there would surely have been a roughhouse if one had appeared in full rig.

For most of us, it was the first time on a ship: for a few, it was the first time away from home. There was a farm labourer from Gloucestershire and his young wife who had never been away from their village—he was emigrating to avoid national service. She had never seen a straw broom before (I think they were uncommon in England) and was deeply intrigued by the notion of cleaning a house with one, eventually borrowing one from the crew to see if she could make it work. In dress and manners they fitted perfectly into that etching of *The Emigrants' Last Look at England* I still have in my basement.

And there was a self-made man with a watch-chain over his belly who entertained everyone in the back bar by actually using all the lingo. "I didn't get where I am by giving my hard-earned money to a lot of layabouts," he said, explaining why he was fleeing the welfare state. "You can't get a decent day's work for a day's pay out of the British working man any more" was another, perhaps the first time I heard it, but exactly the same words as I heard thirty years later in the lounge of the Royal Overseas League. (The speaker, that time, was Australian.) When the question of passing the hat for a tip for the waiters came up, our man said, "Leave me out. I'll look after me and the wife. They'll expect a bit more from me, do you see?" He was probably right.

He was from Lancashire, and by the time we docked, crass remarks in a pseudo-Lancashire accent had become humorous currency in the back bar, when he wasn't there. He performed the familiar catalytic function of absorbing the group's malice, leaving everyone else pleased with each other. He also showed me that life throws up as many clichés as literature. You couldn't put this man into a novel because every literate reader would accuse you of a cheap theft from Dickens.

For three centuries Anticosti Island was the immigrant's first sight of Canada. After that came the day-long journey up the St. Lawrence, waiting for Quebec City to appear. A man in a pointed hat on horseback looked down on us from the Gaspé hills, and I displayed my learning by identifying him as a member of the Royal North-West Mounted Police, which is what he was in the last stories I had read about Canada, tales for an eight-year-old. One of the Canadians thought it more likely he was a scoutmaster having an afternoon jog, and I shut up until I had learned something about this country.

We landed on Dominion Day, 1951, docking at Quebec City, where I got my introduction to the two cultures. The French immigration officer looked at my passport and asked, "You 'ave a job?"

"Not yet," I said. "I just got off the boat."

He looked at me carefully. "How much money?"

I told him. He made me show him.

He walked over to the water-cooler to have a chat with a friend. The two of them shared a laugh; he adjusted his armbands, came back to me, and said, "You realize that if you become a vagrant, we deport you?"

"In chains?"

It was a mistake. "Wait over there," he said.

"I was joking."

"I'm not. Wait over there."

Half an hour later, everyone else in his line having been dealt with, he crooked his finger to signal me back. "Now, my friend, what trade do you 'ave?"

"I'm a clerk." I remembered to pronounce it to rhyme with *jerk*, my first effort at assimilation.

"We 'ave plenty of clerks out of work already."

"Then I might have to do something else." I was beginning to be less intimidated as I realized that even if this man had the power to detain me, or send me back, he would involve himself in a lot of trouble if he did. I just had to let him toy with me for a bit. I had learned that much from the SWOs in the air force.

"What else can you do?" A pure sneer.

"Labourer, dishwasher, road sweeper. Whatever's going."

He sucked his teeth and spat a shred of meat on to the floor.

"You ever done those jobs?"

"All of them."

He walked over to his pal by the cooler, chatted, came back, picked up a newspaper, then, as an afterthought, threw my passport on the table from six feet away so that I had to catch it before it slid off.

"That's it?" I asked.

"Until you fuck up. Then we send you back. You want a piece of advice? Don't stay in Montreal."

Two people from the ship were waiting for me, a nice girl from Sevenoaks, or some such town, who was going to travel with me as far as Winnipeg, on her way to her brother in Calgary, and a Canadian girl, one of the few on board, who had decided to wait in case my brush with the immigration officer got serious.

"What was that all about?" I asked her.

"That was all about your accent and your passport. About Anglo-French relations. That's the way he gets treated in Alberta. It all evens up. Welcome to Canada."

I wasn't dismayed. I was too excited and pleased with myself for having found myself in Canada at all. At this time I was beginning to develop the trick, a fairly common one, I know, of watching myself as an actor in my own drama, and the Quebec dock looked and sounded exotic enough to encourage this. "He stood in the customs shed, hearing the French officials calling to each other, wondering what the new land had to offer him." It was easy to fit a snotty immigration officer into my script. And for another thing, although I couldn't speak French, I *could* speak English, and a lot of people from the *Canberra* who couldn't were having a much harder time being processed than I had had. Most of them were still there when I was through, waiting as they had waited before in the camps many of them had endured to get this far. They were not quite sure what was happening, why they were waiting, foreigners in a foreign land in a way I never was. But they, too, were comfortable within their anxiety. They had made it, too; they just had to be patient for a few hours, and the rest of the future was theirs.

We sailed into Montreal the following morning, took our luggage to the station, and walked around the city until it was time to catch the train. The highlight of the day was a three-egg omelette I ate for lunch in the coffee shop of the train station. It was huge and full of tomatoes and came with home fries and coleslaw and toast, and even after a week on the ship my ration-shrunk stomach still could not get it all in. I decided to wait a while before I tried one of their steaks. And the other thing that came with it was my first cup of North American coffee. After ten years of thinking that coffee meant a spoon of black liquid mixed with hot water, this was a revelation.

That evening we began the journey westward, through northern Quebec and Ontario. For hour after hour we clicked quietly through the forest—pine, mostly, but with a sprinkling of silver birch. I had seen it all on film, but the perspective from inside the train was different. The contrast between the air-controlled, hushed (compared to the clack and bustle of English trains), luxuriously padded environment and the vast, nearly uninhabited bush outside created the impression of being in a wildlife museum, where you look through glass at mock-ups of the animal world. But this was real, and when anything moved outside, I realized that it was us who were behind glass, being viewed by the world out there.

A curve in the track showed you both ends of the train, and beyond the train the national lifeline, the railway, a single track crossing giant trestle bridges, slipping along ledges on the sides of cliffs, moving quietly through the forest. Once, a long way down, a toy cabin appeared on the edge of a lake. A canoe was pulled up on the shore. The tiny figure of a man stood in the doorway of the cabin.

"He's a trapper," the conductor said. "See those frames behind the cabin? He pegs his skins out to dry on those."

The engineer sounded the train's wonderful signal, the little trapper waved, and the tableau was complete, like something arranged by Canadian Pacific to greet new Canadians.

I travelled colonist class, sleeping at an angle of forty-five degrees, sitting up all day in the first-class compartment with the nice girl from Sevenoaks. When I first appeared in her compartment, the conductor tried to send me back to where I belonged but she vouched for me and he let me stay. I bought food from the candy butcher who sold sandwiches, chocolate bars, and coffee, a diet which suited me fine for two days. The girl from Sevenoaks had vouchers for her meals, prepaid by her brother, and she tried to treat me to a meal in the dining car, but I couldn't allow that. One day I would, I thought; one day. It was five years before I came back for the full experience—a sleeper, vouchers of my own, and drinks in the club car. It was worth the wait.

I'm glad I made that trip, and, in time, did the other portions of the transcontinental rail journey. I have the same feeling about the relationship of the railroad to the country as every other sentimentalist. I think everyone who applies for citizenship ought to show they have travelled across the country at least once by train.

Eighteen

Winnipeg

In WINNIPEG I found a room at the YMCA and got a job the next day as a shipping clerk in Gault's Dry Goods Warehouse. I knew all about clerking, I thought, and I turned up for work that first day in Winnipeg in my brown double-breasted suit from Burton's, "the Fifty-Shilling Tailors," and my Austin Reed tie, and found myself part of a group of teenagers dressed in rags. It was my first intimation that I didn't speak the language as well as I thought, because shipping clerk meant labourer and the job consisted of lifting crates of sheets and such around the warehouse and loading them on to trucks. One of the kids took pity on me and found me a set of ragged overalls. By the end of the day I was filthy, and I changed back into my suit feeling like a derelict wearing someone else's cast-offs. I lasted three weeks at the warehouse until I realized I would be better spending my time and my remaining cash looking for a proper job. No one was surprised when I quit. They had my last week's pay ready in half an hour: forty hours at sixty cents an hour, less deductions, for a total of eighteen dollars and change. I took the lads out for a beer just as if I'd been there ten years, and they wished me luck.

The next day I went to the unemployment office and asked for another job. They sent me for an interview with Canada Packers. It took about an hour to find the plant, but there was no mistaking the smell when I got close. A nice, chubby little man in rimless glasses who looked as if he ate a lot of the company's products interviewed me, and arranged for me to be tested. There were three of us being interviewed. First we wrote a general-knowledge test, which asked us to match up pairs like Charles Dickens and *Oliver Twist*. Then there was an arithmetic test, easy enough except for a question involving square root for which I had forgotten the method. Then we had a medical and a tour of the plant. First the sausage machinery, followed by a walk through a sea of blood to the killing floor where we saw and heard the animals dying, and the smell was enough to make a surgeon gag. After that, the little man took us to the cafeteria for lunch, and then we returned to his office where I found out that I had failed and the other two had passed.

Failed what?

"Usually," he said, "we don't release details but in your case I think I can tell you that everything is fine except your square root."

"I forgot the method," I said.

"Everybody at Canada Packers has to know square root," he said. "Why don't you go home, brush up your square root, and come back next week? I'll keep your application on file."

Next I tried out for the job of assistant manager at Kresge's. The man who conducted the interview was very sad, in the sense of unhappy, nearly crying. I sat down facing him across the desk and he took off his glasses carefully, as if they were stuck to his head, and began polishing them, staring at me in near-sighted misery. Then he started the questions.

"Name?"

I told him.

"You out of work?"

"Yes, sir. I just arrived from England."

"You speak English, all right?"

"Yes, sir. All my life."

"A lot of you people don't. Goddam Galicians."

He said nothing more for a long while. Then, "What kind of work have you done?" He put his glasses back on and took a good look at me, pushing himself back from his desk so he could see my feet.

I told him.

"You know what this job entails?"

"No, sir."

"You're the lowest in the store. Even the stock clerk will piss on you. You going to like that?"

I said no, but I understood. He was speaking metaphorically.

"If there's any trouble with the customers, that's your job."

"Yes, sir." What was he talking about? Fights? Riots?

"You have to clean up the dogshit."

"Yes, sir."

"All the crap," he said, getting a bit livelier. "You have to clean up all the crap."

"Yes, sir." A ton a day?

"You prepared to go to Saskatoon?"

Just the way he put it made it unnecessary to ask where Saskatoon was. "No," I said.

That cheered him up. "That's too bad. Send in the other fella on your way out, will you?" He offered me a hand like a piece of tongue, and I left. It was too late for any more interviews so I went back to my room.

When I returned to the unemployment office the next day, the clerk told me that a construction company wanted an accountant. I knew nothing about construction (he meant *building*) and I wasn't an accountant. I was a former clerk with the Asiatic Petroleum Company.

I couldn't do anything, which was why I was in Canada. The clerk looked at his card. "They aren't paying for a real accountant," he said. "And they've been looking for a month. It's in Churchill, see."

"Where's Churchill?"

"Christ knows. Out of town. Up north, I think."

The man at the construction office listened while I told him how little I knew about accounting. "I don't know a debit from a credit," I said.

"Do you drink?" he asked.

"How do you mean?" Was the building site teetotal?

"Are you a lush? An alcoholic?"

"I don't like spirits."

"Jesus, I should hope not at your age."

I meant whisky; he meant methylated spirits, shaving lotion and such.

"Why did you leave England?"

I was used to this question by now. I told him how I wanted to get ahead, how Canada was the land of opportunity, which was what I thought he would want to hear.

He was not impressed. "It's just as easy to fall on your ass here as anywhere else."

The phone rang. He picked it up and listened. "I'm kinda busy now," he said. "I'm just talking to the new guy we're sending to Churchill." He put the phone down. "Okay. You go up on Tuesday. Fifty a week, plus your board and room. Okay?"

It was three times what the warehouse paid, and in Winnipeg I was having to pay fifteen a week for board and room.

"What about the accounting?"

"I could teach you all the accounting this job calls for in ten minutes," he said. "But you might as well wait until you get up there. It'll give you an interest for the first week. It's government contract work and all you have to do is fill in the numbers on their forms and add them up. There's an adding machine up there."

"When do you need me?"

"Now. Tuesday."

"How do I get there?"

He looked at me consideringly, then smiled, more to himself than at me. "You don't have a pot to piss in, right?"

"I'm waiting for my funds to arrive from England." I'd worked out this phrase as a way of explaining to my landlady why I couldn't pay the rent ahead of time. I don't think she believed me, either, but she took a chance.

"I'll bet you are. Here's a voucher that'll get you a ticket." He considered me again and opened a drawer. "Here's something to keep you going. Sign this receipt and send it back to me when your funds arrive from your bankers." He gave me fifty dollars, grinning. "Now take yourself out of here. I'm busy."

Out of the office I looked at the voucher in my hand; it was for a plane ticket. They did things in style in this country, I thought, before I went to the library and looked up Churchill, to find it was six hundred miles north, well beyond the suburbs. I went home, paid my landlady her rent, and prepared to leave.

I was sorry to be leaving Winnipeg so soon. Like everything else in this new world, it was still being something of an Emerald City. About now I was beginning to try to write down some of the things that were happening to me, mainly because I had no money and lots of time, and I felt as if I had woken up after a very long sleep. I have never been a scene-painter—two or three sentences of description are about as much as I can manage, but at that time I accepted that it was the duty of the writer to describe the world as he saw it. I had not yet learned honesty, and what survives in my notebook from those days is embarrassing—doom-laden sentences describing the sunset over Portage Avenue, or the starlit brilliance of the night—stuff like that.

In fact, my impression of Winnipeg was that it consisted of a right angle made by two streets: one arm, Portage Avenue (a name, I understood, which meant that this was the point where you had to pick up your canoe and carry it to Edmonton), went straight west across the Prairies; the other, North Main, went north and then faded into the muskeg.

I did notice the light; though not as brilliant as Calgary's, which is as pure as the light of Greece, in comparison to the miasma that then passed for daylight in coal-burning London, summer and winter, this light hurt. After the light, I noticed the heat, a dry heat, they called it, and so it was compared with the atmosphere on the London Underground in July. Even in my fifty-shilling suit, temperatures which would have been unbearable at home were perfectly manageable here. Besides, there was air-conditioning.

Then there was the food. I had to live carefully until I learned how far my few dollars would go, but even so I ate as I had never eaten before. Hot dogs, hamburgers, chili con carne, pancakes with bacon, pot roast, corned beef hash, navy bean soup, eggs-over-easy, club sandwiches, bologna sausage, banana-cream pie, coconut-cream pie, apple pie à la mode, apple pie with cheese, pumpkin pie, upside-down cake, ham steaks, hot beef sandwiches, coleslaw, Denver sandwiches—I had read about all these foods in Steinbeck, the romantic of the bus depots, and I liked them all except pumpkin pie.

And then there was Child's. I had come looking for drugstores with lunch counters and when I found them they were as satisfying as I had hoped, straight out of movies like *They Drove by Night*, coffee shops with "What'll-it-be?" waitresses named Mae, glasses of ice-cold water (there was no ice in English restaurants), bottomless cups of coffee, and real, working jukeboxes. But the Ritz of all coffee shops was Child's, located properly on the corner of Portage and Main, the centre of the New World, in all its brass-and-redwood magnificence, the classiest lunch counter I have ever known, the sort the *Queen Elizabeth* would have had if it had had a coffee shop in first class, whose tables (two near the window) nightly held all the young intellectuals in Winnipeg, about six or seven then, in talk until midnight. It was an innocent time, a decade before the era when students took all their clothes off the day after they registered at college, and the talk in Child's was a memorable part of it, without dope or acid, but with lots and lots of tobacco and coffee. Later, as students, we ended up in Child's any night we were downtown, but I discovered it for myself that first summer. They should not have demolished it: it was the Café Royale, the Closerie des Lilas, of the tundra.

In those first days, I walked to work in the morning light beside myself with the splendour and rightness of it all, and came home to the wonder of endless hot water in the showers, then walked the streets some more, expectantly. I remember only two flies in the ointment. One night after a week or so I walked up North Main looking for a pub. I had heard they existed, but had never seen the sign of a door into one. A cigar-store clerk pointed to what I was looking for and I walked through a door, down a shallow flight of steps into a scene that was a cross between the drinking den in David Lean's version of *Oliver Twist* and the space bar in *Star Wars*. The noise was the sound of liquid violence; a hundred men sat around tables for four or six or eight, drinking identical glasses of ice-cold beer, all of them shouting, as they had to, some of them sodden drunk, and one or two preparing to slide to the floor, which was swimming in beer. I felt a pang of regret for the cosy saloon bars I had left behind me. This was like the waiting room of a station on the Trans-Siberian railway, with all the waiting passengers trying to get drunk.

The sole purpose of beverage rooms was to get drunk in. Neither the customers nor the management at the time were allowed to sing, and only the waiters were permitted to stand up or walk to another table. There were no women allowed. The idea was to make drink as unattractive as possible, and it worked for me.

The other problem was Sunday. Winnipeg was closed on Sundays. Child's was open, but otherwise the only place to go to was a magazine and newspaper store on Portage Avenue, a few yards west of Child's. But once you had been there, there was nowhere to go except back to Child's, where you could sit and read the three-week-old English newspaper you had bought until the manager told you to leave. Then there was nowhere else to go so you went back to your room and waited for Monday. In England I used to be depressed on Sunday afternoons like everyone else, but at least the day had already contained the Sunday papers and the best dinner of the week, and the cinemas were open in the evening. This was different. This was like a siege. Some years later I heard of a man who got through Winnipeg Sundays by staying in his room and eating yogurt, but he was a philosophy teacher. That kind of serenity was difficult to attain for an immigrant. Even later, when I was a student, the problem was still there. Some students formed a film club with the object of getting around the regulations prohibiting public entertainment on Sundays, and I joined immediately, but the movie the first night in the basement of United College was *L'Atalante* without subtitles and so poorly lit that it seemed to have been printed on brown paper, so I gave up. I speculated later that the reason that everyone in Winnipeg, and, for all I knew, everyone west of Montreal, ate Sunday dinner at night was to give themselves something to look forward to all day.

But except for the beverage rooms and Sundays, I liked Winnipeg, and I have thought of myself ever since as a Manitoban who has come east to Toronto, like everyone else I knew at the university. Lately, we hear, Winnipeg has the highest crime rate in Canada, but they've got a lot of catching up to do. It was a very innocent town once.

The following Tuesday I climbed into the DC-3 which flew me to Churchill with stops at Dauphin and The Pas. The plane was full of construction workers, and when she heard my accent the stewardess sat with me for most of the flight because she wanted to talk about a book she was reading, *Brideshead Revisited*, which she was finding weird. I hadn't read it—it was only just published—but we soon found something we had both read, *Cold Comfort Farm*, I think, and I had a fine time flying north. That was the last stewardess who had time to talk to me.

Nineteen

Gateway to the Arctic

THEY CALLED Churchill the "Gateway to the Arctic," a former Hudson's Bay fur-trading post, at one time an outpost of the Empire protected from the French by the garrison of Fort Prince of Wales. In the thirties, a railway was built, and a port, to ship prairie grain out of Hudson's Bay, but the season is too short to be economic. The Hudson's Bay Company store sold ladies' panties comically emblazoned with the town's slogan, but there were no tourists to buy them. There was a train twice a week; sometimes we went into the town to see it arrive, to watch the porter put down his little steps and call "Churchill!" as if the train had not stopped at the edge of the world. The plane came in on Tuesdays and Thursdays; there was no road.

Most of the time the place is uninhabitable. For about six weeks there is the illusion of summer, days warm enough for shirtsleeves, and nights only a few hours long. But the natives bet newcomers that there will be snow every month, and they usually win. Winter, which begins in September, is merciless; there were weeks when we lived entirely indoors. True, the northern lights crackled across the winter sky like sheets of light being shaken over the world below, but the travel writers who describe this phenomenon move on the next day; it isn't enough to make the whole winter interesting. And then with the first breath of spring, in late May or June, come the flies; first the blackflies in thick nostril-choking swarms, then the mosquitoes making it impossible to work outside without gloves, head-nets, and smudge pots.

I quickly got to hate it, and when I had spent a year there and saw the next winter coming round I had already made my plans to leave. I have ever since been baffled by the talk of the lure of the North, although it undeniably exists; I met men there who could live nowhere else. I suppose the desert has the same effect on the people who live there, and we are more familiar with the romance of it, but what I saw in Churchill was a barren land, lightly covered in unattractive vegetation, muskeg, without colour or smell, a killing bottle of a landscape. Even the seashore of the Bay seemed without life; I tried to walk along the shore as on Brighton beach, looking for what the tide had left behind, but the rock pools were empty. White whales would surface, and in winter there was the occasional polar bear, far out on the ice, so that you knew this land supported life, but it seemed sterile to me. There was one huge eruption of the animal world that winter when the caribou chose to walk through the camp on their annual migration south, thousands of them quietly plodding past the windows for several days, but there seemed no smaller wildlife, and hardly any vegetation to fill the giant spaces. So deprived were our senses that when we flew south we felt assaulted by the jungly fecund smell of the grass at Winnipeg airport.

Apart from the migrating caribou, the only other excitement occurred in the spring when the ice broke up in the Nelson River. On that day, we all piled into trucks and drove into town to watch.

But it was only nature that was vile. In all other ways it was a major piece of luck for me to spend my first year in Churchill because I got a crash course in Canadian culture and history, and after a month I forgot I was English for most of the time, absorbed into the community, into Canada itself, without effort. Everyone at Churchill was an outsider, so I was no lone new stranger in town. We lived communally, in army barracks, depending on our "rank." At first, with the status of a sort of corporal, I was given a bunk in the sub-foremen's room, which I shared with three middle-aged plumbers. We each had a steel bed, and a hook to hang our clothes on, and we kept the rest of our gear in a box under the bed. It was just like the air force.

We were building a military station on the famed Distant Early Warning line, a system that was supposed to give warning of Russian attacks by air from the north. The plumbers and steam-fitters were there to make as much money in as short a time as possible. It was the only thing we had in common. My roommates, the sub-foremen, were responsible family men who stayed out of the beer parlour to save their money. But apart from the beer parlour and the game of poker in the main bunkhouse, there was nothing to do in Churchill except read and talk, and so they told stories while I lay in bed and listened like a child.

It was early days and I was very much in love with a romantic notion of Canada, telling myself that I really was in the Arctic, and I was fascinated by these men and their stories, of their wartime experiences, of the places they had worked, of the Depression—two of them had ridden the rails in search of work—and most of all, of the houses they had built for themselves at different times.

I had never met anyone who had built his own house. Where I came from no one even owned a house; you either rented from a landlord who had thrown up an "estate" of cheap maisonettes as an investment, like Colwood Gardens, or from the municipality who built houses to contain the overflow of the poor from places like Lambeth. Either way, repairs were the responsibility of the landlord, and the householder had no incentive to acquire skills beyond a bit of painting and gardening. Even the plumbers, the bricklayers, and the carpenters we knew at home did not dabble in another man's trade.

But these men had done it all, sometimes including clearing the land before they built their houses, plumbed them, wired them, dug their own wells, and laid out septic fields. They were, or were directly descended from, homesteaders, another romantic word, and I was thrilled to find myself among them. I felt I was hearing stories of the old West, too late for me, but I was in time to at least hear about it first-hand from the sons of the pioneers themselves.

In a few weeks the construction manager got me reclassified from corporal (or sub-foreman) to sergeant and I moved to the sergeants' mess, where the rest of the clerks, the timekeepers, and the storekeepers were billeted. I was happy to move because I got my own room, and the mess had a lounge and a bar and a pool room, but I should have stayed with the sub-foremen and completed my education at night.

I used to wonder why I did not become an alcoholic in Churchill. I certainly have an addictive personality, beginning at five years old with "Tizer" and coconut ice, and continuing through cigarettes to, now, four or five kinds of food—clam chowder, Russian bread, gravlax, navy bean soup—all of which I eat too much of when I can get them. Certainly I drank far more in Churchill than I was used to, beginning the week with a bottle of beer on Tuesday night and climaxing in a roaring drunk on Saturday night at the dance in the mess. On Sunday and Monday I stayed out of the bar and tried to lead a better life, ironing my shirts, writing letters home, and reading self-improvement books.

There wasn't a great deal else to do but drink, especially in the winter which lasted most of the year. Like any northern outpost, Churchill attracted a lot of people, particularly in the construction trades, for whom a job in the North was a last chance to straighten out their lives and save some money. But Churchill was no place to come to, to get away from liquor, and it was here that I gained the impression that all Canadian workmen routinely went on a tear about once a month and stayed drunk for a week. I think even in Churchill such cases made up a very small minority of the crew, but they made a strong impression on me. In the city they would have been fired the first time they were found drunk on the job, but skilled tradesmen were hard to attract up there, and they got several chances to fall off the wagon.

The sober plumbers and fitters were up there to make money, lots of it; they were guaranteed a forty-eight-hour week for which they were paid for fifty-six hours, plus free board and room and a free flight to Winnipeg every three months. If they worked Saturday afternoon, they were paid double time, and on Sundays, triple time. In six months, I heard a plumber say, you could save up the down payment on a house, whatever that was.

There was a cinema on camp whose program changed three times a week; there was a dance of some kind in the officers' mess on Saturday night, and another in the sergeants' mess, and there was the local version of the Manitoba beverage room for the other ranks and civilian workers. There was friction occasionally between the civilian workers and the soldiers, and between the Canadian Army and the Americans, and this tension usually came to a head in the beer parlour. One night a member of the Royal 22nd Regiment, the famous "Van Doos," did his celebrated belly dance on a tabletop in the beer parlour. One of the American soldiers made a jeering remark, suggesting, against all the evidence, that the Canadian soldier was effeminate, and the resulting brawl lasted, I was told, for an hour before the military police could control it.

There were twenty or thirty girls on the camp—clerks, typists, and scientific workers—up there doing some kind of classified work for the Defence Research Board. Most of the classified studies had to do with the cold, I think. There was even a detachment of the navy, a petty officer and two or three ratings, doing something mysterious with a motor launch in Hudson Bay.

It was hard to stay amused and sober. One day a notice went up announcing the formation of the Churchill Little Theatre, inviting anyone interested to join. I went along to the first meeting, was soon made director because I had seen some plays in the West End, and profited by finding a way to fill in my evenings that winter in the company of some very agreeable people. But when I turned *The Monkey's Paw*, W. W. Jacob's horror story, into a rollicking farce, I cured myself of any notion that I could act in or direct anything above the level of a village pageant.

We had already produced two plays that winter and now we decided that our third production would consist of three one-act plays, two comedies and a melodrama. The decision to put on the two comedies first may have started the trouble because when the curtain went up on *The Monkey's Paw*, the final offering, the audience was still chuckling from the comedies. They continued to chuckle through the first two scenes of the melodrama because they had had no sign from the stage that this wasn't another comedy. They were always a supportive audience. And then in the third scene, as the melodrama turned to farce, they became hysterical.

The story from which the play is adapted is well known. A soldier has brought back from the East a magic paw which has the power to grant its owner three wishes, but in a way to make the owner regret making them. In the play, a family of Mother, Father, and their son Herbert have wished for two hundred pounds to pay off their mortgage. The wish is granted: Herbert gets caught in his factory's machinery and the family is compensated for his death with the sum of two hundred pounds.

Then Mother gets the idea of using one of the remaining wishes in the paw to bring Herbert back. Father reluctantly makes the wish and immediately there is a thump on the door as the play moves into its climax. I was playing Father, and I had procured a reasonable-looking monkey's paw from the army kitchen in the shape of a turkey's foot which one of the cooks shaped into the likeness of a paw. An additional note of tension was added in our production when I dropped the claw early in the scene and it slid across the stage to fall with a clang into the footlights which were recessed and about a foot back from the edge of the stage. The front row was full of army cooks, come to see the part that their claw was playing in our skit, as they called it, and when I dropped the claw into the footlights they leaned forward, gleefully, knowing I would have to get that claw back.

Quickly, the pounding at the door becomes loud and continuous; Mother is calling for Herbert to be let in, but I, fearful of letting in Herbert's mangled corpse, am scrabbling around on my knees, looking for the paw to use the last wish to send Herbert back to the grave.

Now the weaknesses in the dialogue became apparent. I think we had written our own version and whoever had transposed the third scene had no ear for the absurd effects of unintentional rhyme. The result was something like this:

Mother: (*Struggling with the cardboard scenery*) I can't find the
lock to open the door. Wait, Herbert, I'm coming.
Me: (*On my knees*) There's one more wish. I must find
the paw!
Mother: The door!
Me: The paw!
Mother: The door! The door!
Me: The paw! The paw!
Mother: I can't open the door!
Me: I can't find the paw!

It was by now apparent to the whole audience that I would eventually have to walk over to the footlights to pick out that claw. When I finally did, the cooks in the front row were laughing hysterically, punching each other with tears running down their faces. I made my wish as Mother flung open the door. Two or three seconds later someone switched on the moonlight to show that there was nothing there and we dropped the curtain on *The Monkey's Paw*.

Like the sober construction workers, I was saving a lot of money. Beer, I think, was twenty-five cents a bottle and the Saturday night double whiskies were fifty cents. I was given two raises in a year and after I had bought underwear and socks there was nothing to spend my money on, and I saved fifty dollars a week with no effort at all. A friend from England, Tony Harold, followed me out to Canada in January and I flew down to Winnipeg where he met me off the plane and we took a large room at the Marlborough Hotel and had a fine week together, eating in Child's three times a day and spending our evenings at the movies. I had found a job for Tony in Churchill, but he resisted the lure of the North, so I lent him some money until he could find a job and went back up by myself.

Returning to the camp after visiting the civilized delights of Winnipeg caused me to ponder the future in search of some decisions. I had emigrated effectively, and found my freedom; now it was time to do something with it. Through the Little Theatre, I had met several recent graduates of the University of Manitoba, and one in particular, Ian Croll, took on the now-vacant role of mentor, and made me aware that I might be able to get back into the educational stream that I thought I had left for ever when I joined the Asiatic Petroleum Company. This sounded like a lark. I was twenty-two. I still had no large ambitions, not even for a degree. What I saw was an opportunity, finally, an excuse, to read books for a year without having to explain myself to people like my family. I could easily save a thousand dollars by September, and my Churchill friends assured me that a thousand dollars would be enough for tuition, board and room, a couple of Hathaway shirts, and a Hanford-Drewitt jacket, everything I would need to impersonate a student. I wrote to the Universities of Toronto and Manitoba to find out what my School Certificate was worth and was accepted by both. Toronto was willing to give me direct entrance into second year, so I chose Manitoba as the institution that best knew what it was doing.

Spring was coming, but winter made one last try and almost got one of our plumbers. His truck had broken down, and no one missed him for a few hours: he should not have been out at all as all vehicles had been ordered off the road. When they eventually found him he was nearly gone. Forty years later, out of the memory of that incident I got a short story, "One of a Kind." Reading it now, I think it should be called "Snow," but that is true of any story I could write about Churchill.

Twenty

News from England

IN APRIL the sun returned, the ice cracked in the Nelson River, the blackflies and mosquitoes swarmed once more, and I began to look forward to the fall. Mark Gokel, a corporal in the American army and a stalwart of the Little Theatre, had suggested he and I hitchhike down to his home in South Dakota from Winnipeg, which seemed like a good idea in 1952, and we left early in August. Mark wore his uniform and we had no trouble getting rides down to Minneapolis, his old stamping ground, where an aunt loaned him her car and we drove up to the Minnesota lake country where some of his friends had summer cabins, and spent a pleasant couple of days at the lake. From there we travelled back to his home in Sioux Falls, South Dakota, where I was introduced to the, I think, Midwestern custom of eating slices of ripe tomatoes sprinkled with sugar, a dessert that was probably invented in the Depression; I had never seen it in England, but we didn't have tomatoes of that size. I like it for its newness, but when I tried it again back in Winnipeg it tasted like a way to get children to eat vegetables. Then we thumbed our way back to Winnipeg, where we parted, he back to Churchill and me to the Fort Garry campus of the University of Manitoba.

I was glad to have left Churchill. It had been the best possible experience for me: Because of the mixed nature of the community, I had had a crash course in Canadian society and history, learning about such things as the prairie dust bowl of the thirties from a sometime farmer, about how much the English were disliked in the Depression in Toronto (a real shock this, learning of the signs on factory gates: NO ENGLISH NEED APPLY), of the Depression itself, so much more severe apparently than the English "slump" I had grown up in; I had roomed with a man who rode the rails looking for work, staying in hobo camps, and another who hated the fabled Mounties for their strike-breaking history; found out something about the ethnic diversity of a country I had assumed was half English and half French, and about the animosities that confirmed that diversity. (I had a girlfriend for a while who told me that once, on a summer job, she had been called a "goddam hunky-dogan" by a supervisor. She had to explain to me that "hunky" meant Ukrainian, and a "dogan" was a Catholic.) I had worked, voluntarily and out of curiosity, for a week as a steam-fitter's helper, wearing a mosquito net, wrestling with lengths of pipe that were heavy beyond my strength, learning that there are kinds of physical labour every manager should experience personally before being allowed to lay down the working conditions of the labour crew.

And most of all I had saved a thousand dollars and earned the right to read books for a year. Paradise. In fact, I was picking up where I had left my law-student air force pal, drinking tea in his rooms at Oxford. Then, I was rubbing my nose against the glass that separated that world from what was possible for me. Now, I was going through the door. I expected the University of Manitoba to be every bit the experience I imagined Oxford to be, and it was. In 1952, most youths who grew up in Canada in circumstances parallel to mine—one of a family of ten, say, on a farm in the Saskatchewan dust bowl—would have been just as unlikely to regard university as a possibility as I did in England. I was privileged now, and I knew it. I also knew how lucky I was to find myself in first year in James Reaney's English class, the most engrossing experience of its kind since Mr. Thomas trained me for the scholarship exam. Reaney's class was what I had imagined studying literature would be like, and although I never had a learning experience like that again, it was enough to confirm that I was where I wanted to be.

I still had some explaining to my family to do. My cover story was that I was enrolling in the bachelor of commerce program, which was true, because in first year it was identical to the B.A. program. I learned later that my brother explained to the others that I was probably thinking of going into the insurance business. It says something about my relationship to my family that I should have felt obliged to construct this story about a bachelor of commerce. Obviously it was a concession to the old values, central to which was the getting and holding of a steady job. An arts degree meant nothing to them, but a commerce degree would enable Joe to assure my mother, the guardian of those values, that I was on the right track. And perhaps there was a trace of guilt at having left home just when my wages would have been useful to the family. I certainly felt guilty about something.

And some part of the reason was that my mother regularly, though not naggingly or insistently, was the one who raised the question of when I was coming home, to remind me that this Canada thing was just temporary until I settled down. A degree in commerce took five years, so that merely enrolling in such a program sent a message that going home was not a very high priority with me any more, but I was still interested in a steady job.

And then, at Christmas in the first year, Joe sent a telegram to say that my mother had died, victim of the London smog that affected so many that year. When I got the news, I walked the streets of Winnipeg all night, trying to think. Although there was never much expression of emotion in the family, I found out now that the emotion itself was there, but that I didn't know how to express it. I sent a telegram back to my brother, revealing enough. "What do I do, now?" was all I said, and he replied consolingly. There was no question of my being able to go home in time for the funeral, although, astonishingly, a man named Lorne Sinclair, a man I hardly knew who was a friend of Tony's (my friend from England with whom I now shared a garrett on Donald Street), offered to lend me the air fare if I wanted to go. But it was an enormous amount of money, and I didn't see how I could pay it back, and there was nothing to go home for.

A week later I wrote the end-of-term exams, still very numb. I went to see the dean afterwards, and asked that the results be set aside because I couldn't remember writing the exams, but he told me to wait and see and the results turned out to be about what I would have expected. And then it was Christmas, and I began to think of other things.

The other effect of her death was that I was now free. For a year and a half I had been visiting Canada, more or less under the assumption that I would return home when I had got "it" out of my system. Now that cord was cut. Joe assured me that my father would be taken care of by my sister who would take over the house, and I made a tentative plan to go home when I graduated and see them all.

I have no doubt that any psychologist would be able to analyse the nature of the bond between my mother and the rest of us. A sister-in-law once said to me, accurately enough, "You Wrights are not a very affectionate family but you do know your duty." Both of these qualities flowed from my mother, I think. She fed us, taught us manners, clothed us, and repaired us, mostly by taking us up to St. Thomas's Hospital as required.

I don't think she had time or energy for anything more. Bringing ten children into the world was a duty, and caring for them, in the sense of looking after them, was another. But the attachment was very strong, even if it didn't show itself in displays of affection. The night

I left I was too selfishly preoccupied to take much notice of her response, but I think now that she had not wanted to face the good-byes, that night or the next morning. She had cried the time I asked if I could join the merchant navy, taking my wish to leave as some kind of failure on her part. Perhaps she had also felt my leaving for Canada to be her own failure.

Most of all, I think, by the time I knew her well, she was worn out. She had no energy for her grandchildren, for example. So long as they were well behaved she was nice to them, found sweets for them in her purse, and so on. But when a daughter approached her with the idea of babysitting her children for an afternoon, pointing out that all her friends' mothers did it, my mother became raucous. "Look after your kids, you mean? While you go out gallivanting. Who am I, then? Muggins? Brought up ten of me own and finally get half an hour to meself and you want me to look after this pair? You must need your head examined."

She was the centre of power in the house and when she died the power went, too. I wrote to her automatically and regularly while she was alive, but after her death I may have written to my father once or twice, but no more. He wasn't a letter-writing man, belonging to a generation and a class that did not have the habit. I used to get messages from him occasionally. The telephone would ring and it would be the daughter of a mate of his at his stable, just passing through, reporting that he was all right, and I would give them a message to take back that I was, too. And Stan Yass, with whom I was in regular correspondence, took it upon himself to drop by the house in Colwood Gardens every few months and send me a report. (Stan, I learned much later, liked and admired my mother. Even when we were sixteen, he had found the idea of ten children amazing, and, more than my other friends, he always sought her out in the kitchen to pay his respects. In her turn, she liked to see him call, always letting us use the front room, and pressing tea on him. "Nicely dressed," she said of him once. "Well-spoken," she said another time. "Always polite" was another, and "He must come from a good family," and finally, her highest accolade, "Very genuine," which it would take an essay to explicate.)

So I began to write to Joe, not very often but whenever a major event, like my graduation or my marriage, needed to be communicated. And he wrote back a periodic chronicle letter when enough events had piled up to make a letter worthwhile. And then, somewhere in there, the working class in England began to get telephones—there was no telephone in the house before my mother died—and after that a rare telephone call and Christmas cards kept us in touch.

Twenty-One

The Bridge

I CONTINUED to make enough money in the summer to pay for the winter, mainly because every summer I found a construction job in a remote area, with my fare to and from the site and board and room thrown in. My career as a construction worker only came to an end in the summer before my final year when the company I worked for got into difficulties.

The job was plagued with problems, and the solutions only created more problems. The on-site management disintegrated as the blame for our mistakes searched for someone to attach itself to, until by August there was only one foreman left, and me.

I had been sent up because of my experience as a storekeeper and timekeeper, told on no account to interfere with the foreman, but to keep track of the money we were spending. When I appeared and tried to explain my mission, the foreman grasped the half-truth that I had been sent up to spy, and reacted accordingly.

His tactic for dealing with me was to treat me as his boss. This was absurd, but it had a kind of logic. On my first morning on the job, after he had sized me up, he asked, "Will I tell the fitter to begin the test on the twelve-inch line from the officers' mess?"

He knew that I hadn't the faintest idea what he was talking about. I tried a joke. "I don't know. Will you?"

"It's you I'm asking," he said. "You're the boss."

It was clear he was up to something, but I wasn't sure what. "I'm just here to count the spare material and make up the payroll," I said.

"Yez don't work for me."

"No. Not really."

"Then I must be working for you. There's no one else about. Shall I turn on the twelve-inch steam?"

I told myself to play dumb, to assume that in asking the question of me, in treating me as his boss, Phil Jennings was genuinely seeking an answer. He was just asking the wrong man. But I knew where to find the right one.

"I'll phone head office," I said.

He looked at me without expression, trying to figure out whether I had made a brilliant move, or stumbled accidentally on the only way of handling the situation. He nodded and sat down and I picked up the phone and waited for the girl at the switchboard to ask me for a number.

Jennings stood up. "P'raps you'd better not bother," he said. "I'll take a chance, seeing as *you* can't because you don't know. Yez can't be botherin' your superiors every time you want to go to the toilet. They'd expect you to take a little responsibility."

Much later I realized that I had lighted by chance on the best way to handle him. He had to take me off the hook sooner than he had planned because the owners knew their trade and they would have responded by asking Jennings what he was playing at; obviously it was his decision and he should get on with it. At the time it began to seep through to me only that something had happened to my advantage. I wasn't sure what it was, but I thought I knew how to make it happen again.

Next I asked him for the use of the truck to get round the site to find the material I was sent to look for. He thought I should hire my own. "That truck's me own personal property, d'ye see. Better get yourself a four-wheel drive," he said.

I reached for the phone.

"Hold on, now. Hold on. I'd a thought you had the authority to provide yourself with a little bit of transportation."

"No, Phil, no. No authority for things like that." I picked up the phone.

"In that case, you'd better use my truck until we see how it goes."

Which is what the office would have told me to do, since they were paying him for the use of his truck.

And so it went for the next two weeks. Several more times he tried to box me in, but as each time I reached without shame for the phone, each time he made the decision himself, shaking his head in disgust at my feebleness.

And then the balloon went up, and I discovered that I was in charge after all.

To understand what happened next it is necessary to know that the site was serviced by a road that ran around the perimeter, and by two other roads that crossed at right angles, like a giant hot cross bun. In spite of the foreman's best efforts, our part of the work was very much behind schedule, and we were now holding up most of the other contractors on the site because of a failure to install a major water line on time. The line had to be laid now, before any more work could go ahead. But to complete the line we had to cut the perimeter road with a trench. But *that* would mean that no one would be able to get round the site until the line was completed, tested, and the trench filled in. Ten days, Jennings, the foreman, estimated. So, quite without guile, he asked me what we should do. Cutting ditches across roads was outside his authority.

I asked him what *he* would do, and he said he didn't have the faintest idea. "It was a consequence of the way the job had been run from the start," he said. "Perhaps we should really call the office, this time, and let them have the problem."

When I called the city, there was no one in our head office except the little old lady who had been kept on from the days when she was all the staff they needed to add up the wages. She said I should do the best I could and trust in the Lord. I put the phone down and looked at Jennings whose face was expressing a mixture of amusement at my predicament and tiredness at his own.

"What are yez going to do, boss?" he asked. He still didn't mean the "boss," of course, but his tone was friendly. This had nothing to do with plumbing or steam-fitting. I was as qualified to understand the implications, and to be as frightened of them, as he was.

I searched for guidance, but there was nowhere I could turn to for help, within my experience or outside it. It was a coin-toss. "Cut the road," I said.

Now it was his problem. He had to decide whether to join me, oppose me, or keep his distance. He looked at me like a man who planned finally to tell me exactly what he thought of me. Fixing me in his sights, he said, "We'll do it first thing in the morning when no one's about. We'll use one of the independent shovel operators. No need to bother the contractors with this. Yet."

So on Sunday morning at six, a giant shovel bit into the only road on the site, and by ten the labour crew were trimming the sides of the trench and Jennings was wondering what the contractors would say when they arrived on Monday.

The next morning the road leading up to the trench looked like one of the beaches at Dunkirk. There was a line of gravel trucks pointing towards the trench, and closer to the ditch about a dozen pick-up trucks and winch trucks with A-frames were scattered about where they had driven off the road to park. A group of men were clustered on the edge of the trench, and about twenty others were lying about on the ground, smoking and grazing, waiting for orders. As I got up to them, the group by the ditch saw me and came at a run. Their spokesman, one of the construction superintendents, a man called Bullock, a one-eyed man who was permanently pissed off on the best of days, shouted, "Who ordered you to do this?"

"No one," I said. "I did it by myself."

I thought he was going to have a stroke. He had very strange breath, sweet and sugary. The rest of him was hot and nasty, from his egg-bald head with the empty eye-socket down to his neck which was all swollen and thick-veined, and looked from behind, as one of the labourers pointed out, like a giant's penis.

"You did it!" he screamed. "You know what you've done?"

"I've cut the trench to put in the steam line to connect up the jobs you people want done," I said. (And these are the men who will put in the pipe that will—etc.)

"You little Limey asshole," he said, and I thought, that's the first time I've heard it. Not asshole; Limey. I'd been called a goddam DP by a plumber we had had to let go, but this was the first time anyone had called me English. It was something I was beginning to forget for weeks at a time.

"What's the trouble?" I asked.

Now he looked as if he was going to boil over. He shoved his face at me and shouted. It was like standing by the exhaust fan of a chocolate factory. "You've brought this whole site to a standstill, you stupid goddam cocksucker," he said. His face was contorted as if someone was pouring hot oil all over his feet. All round us were the people who wanted to cross the ditch. In the trench itself, the labour crew were shovelling and tidying up, watching the show and loving it.

"We're not going to get very far like this, are we?" I said, and turned away.

Bullock screamed. Soon bubbles would be coming out of his ears. "I'll fill the fucking ditch in myself," he bawled. "Charlie, bring your bulldozer over here and start filling in the ditch. You guys"—to our crew—"get out of there."

The labour foreman looked at me for confirmation.

Everyone waited. Jennings had moved closer to me. He said, "Youse fellas carry on unless he tells you different." He pointed to me.

The boys went back to work.

Bullock shouted to Charlie. "Fill the fucking ditch *in*! They'll move or get buried."

Charlie shrugged and stayed where he was. Then Phil said to me, "I suggest you continue the conversation in the office, sir. Let these fellas get on with their work." He pointed to our labour crew.

"Right," I said. "Let's go back to the office and talk about it."

When we were all inside, I said, "So, what's all the excitement?" It was my only line.

One of them undertook to tell me. "In the last week," he said, "as of last Friday, we had one road around the perimeter to serve the whole site. It was a one-way road, not wide enough to take traffic both ways, but we could manage." He was talking to me like an idiot, as if *I* was an idiot. "Now you've cut the perimeter road, nothing can move. You've stopped the camp dead."

Now I realized exactly what I had done. "We have to finish the trench and get that line connected," I said.

"That line is three weeks late. Any time in the last three weeks we could have managed. Now we can't."

"What can we do?"

"Find someone who knows what he's doing? In the meantime, now that you know what you've done, perhaps you would fill in the ditch and wait until another road is built before you dig it out again. BUT YOU CAN'T CUT THE BLOODY ROAD! Now I won't bury your men, but I will ask someone in Ottawa to keep the site clear while I fill in that ditch and I'll do it first thing tomorrow."

The others liked this and they all left, nodding, looking like a hanging posse.

I was left with Jennings and the labour foreman. "What am I going to do?" I asked them.

Jennings said, "Could we build a bypass road?"

The labour foreman said, "It would need to be about three hundred yards long to go round the swamp. It would have to have rock on the bottom, then smaller stones, and then gravel. You'd need eighteen or twenty loads of rock to start, and then . . ."

"All right, all right." It sounded like the Alaska Highway. "How long will it take?"

"I would think if you had six gravel trucks and fifty men, you might build a simple road in a week. I don't know anything about road building. But it will take a week, anyway."

Once again I searched for inspiration, but this time there was an answer. I found myself thinking of my brother Ron, the only relative who worked in construction, and I wondered what he would think of my predicament if he were here, and thinking of Ron freed me to make up an answer. I said, "A bridge?"

"A what?"

"A bridge. We need a bridge."

"You know how to build a bridge?" Jennings asked me. He was grinning openly, and now the labour foreman started to look amused, too. They weren't laughing at me; they were just enjoying not being responsible for a giant screw-up. It was a lark, now.

They both looked at me, waiting.

"Planks?" I asked. "Lay some planks across?"

The labour foreman giggled. "Those gravel trucks weigh twenty tons."

"Big planks?" I was feeling light-headed.

"How big?" Phil asked.

"How big do planks come?"

"Twelve inches."

"How thick?"

"As thick as you like."

"Up to what?"

"Twelve inches."

"The trench is six feet wide," I said. "If we laid twelve twelve-by-twelves across the ditch, would that take a gravel truck?"

"That's pretty solid all right," the foreman said.

"What would happen if the bridge broke?"

"The truck would fall into the ditch and it would take six of them trucks with A-frames to pull it out," Jennings said. "Humpty-fucking-Dumpty."

"I move we build a bridge of twelve twelve-by-twelves across the ditch," I said. "All those in favour, raise your hands."

Phil started to laugh. "Listen to the little fart," he said, meaning me. "You know what you're doing?"

"No, but no one else does, either. You guys are useless." I was giddy with decision-making, a better high than I ever got on dope, later.

"I wasn't trained in the science of bridge-building," Phil said. "I don't have me papers in it." He winked at the labour foreman in a way to frighten horses.

So it was a game.

"Right," I said, to the labour foreman. "Here's an order." I made out an invoice for the lumber we needed.

He said, "If you lay them across the ditch, they'll separate and the wheels will go through them."

"So what do we do?" Now that I had made the big decision, I could ask them to make all the rest without losing any status.

Jennings said. "Cross planks. Git twelve two-by-twelves as well and twenty pounds of spikes. We'll nail them across the timbers."

The foreman said, "When the first truck hits the edge, it'll push the whole thing into the ditch. We'll have to make it flush with ground level. I'll get the crew to cut out bays, twelve feet by three and a foot deep, one on each side. We'll lay the twelve-by-twelves in them and nail the planks across."

Now everyone was thinking.

"Right," I said. "Off we go."

Phil said, "When will we do it?"

"Now. That's what it's all about."

So it was settled. The foreman went for lumber, Jennings organized his helpers into a team, and I went over to the trench to tell the boys what was happening, and to mark out the cut we had to make on the bank. We had a couple of men digging out the bank when the foreman returned with the lumber, accompanied by Bullock.

"I've heard about your idea," Bullock said, breathing his candy-factory breath. "Do you know how much stress twelve-by-twelves will take?"

"No."

"I do. Do you know how much a gravel truck fully loaded weighs?"

"No."

"I do. Now, I don't want to hold you up, so I'll lend you a gravel truck when you're ready. You'll need a driver, though. I wouldn't order one of my men to do it." He sat down on the blade of a bull-dozer to watch.

It took us an hour to cut the bays for the timbers, and another hour to lay the timbers in place and nail the planks over them. By four o'clock, when we had finished, there were about a hundred people watching. Bullock was right—there was no other work going on. When the bridge was ready to be tested there were three opinions, or rather two opinions and one "don't know." The group led by Bullock jeered from start to finish. There was no way, they said, that a structure like that would support a gravel truck. A second, smaller group thought it might work, for a while. The majority were as ignorant as I was, and they were willing to see it happen before they saw that whatever did happen had been obvious from the start.

Among the "pro" group was a truck driver, one of the independents, who offered to make a test run, after Bullock had made him recite the fact that he was not being ordered to do so. At the last minute, Jennings climbed up into the cab with the driver to show his faith in the bridge. My mate.

Twelve-by-twelves are like big wooden matches. They have a little give in them, and then they crack. When the front wheels of the truck rested on the plank, the bridge gave a grunt, but not much happened until the back wheels were over the centre of the bridge. The whole thing bent into a shallow bow and made a lot of cracking noises. The driver kept going and climbed slowly through the cracking sounds and then over the far side, up on to the bank. The bridge returned to its normal shape, and the cracking had not been important.

The crowd stirred and talked together while a second truck, the first in line, went over, this time with hardly any cracking but with the same bowing in the middle. Then a truck with an A-frame went over as though the bridge were made of concrete, and then the other drivers began to start up their engines, explaining to each other that that much timber would support anything, they had seen it before.

Bullock shouted, "You use this at your own risk," but that didn't deter anyone. He walked over to the bridge. "Twelve-by-twelves would never do it by themselves," he said. "The reason it works is that your twelve-by-twos are spreading the load."

"That's right," I said.

Bullock got in his pick-up and raced it across the bridge, nearly skidding off it.

"I'll put up a six-by-six as a guard rail either side," Jennings announced, grinning. "Then even fellas with one eye will be all right."

We worked with the bridge for the rest of the week. That section of the line had to be laid, welded, and then tested under pressure. We couldn't have a crew in the trench while the bridge was being used, so we worked around it during the day and worked a lot of overtime when the rest of the construction had stopped, for time and a half all round. Generally we worked until dark, about nine o'clock. The weather stayed dry. On Friday, Jennings turned the steam on, and on Saturday we came back and the test was holding, so that was all right. The labour crew worked the rest of the day and Sunday, dismantling the bridge and filling in the trench, so that on Monday I was able to report to Bullock that he had his road back. We'd only held them up for one day.

On Monday I said to Jennings, "What happens next? If they don't come back from Ottawa with something soon, we haven't solved anything, have we?"

"Nor will we, me lad. I enjoyed helpin' you build your little bridge, but this job's banjaxed, kaput, finis. You'll see. Me, I've saved a few bucks, and I'm going to have a little holiday. Then I hear there's a demand for the trade out in B.C., some new air force base. You should think about that for yourself. I would imagine they need clerks, too. You can give me as a reference."

He was right, of course. But the summer was almost over and I had a lot of overtime pay coming, so not long after that I took the bus to the city where I bought a shirt with buttons on the collar, and a pair of Daks trousers because all my life I had wanted to own a pair of Daks, and I could finally afford them, and a smashing pair of loafers, and a new sports jacket. A whole new skin. I got my hair cut and stood in the shower for a long time to wash away the rest of Black Lake.

When I was clean and dressed, I went down to the beer parlour in the hotel to have a think about whether to go back to Winnipeg by train, bus, or air. I could afford any of them.

Twenty-Two

Licensed Guide

IN THE 1955-56 academic year I shared an apartment with Bob Rodgers, another English major, who worked in the summers as a guide at a fly-in fishing lodge fifty miles north of Kenora. (Our living arrangement worked well except that sometimes I woke Bob up, shouting, "Len, Len, for Christ's sake, get up." When I told him who Len was, Bob wondered if I was homesick, but I felt no pangs.) He suggested that when we graduated I might apply for a job for the summer as a guide at the fishing camp where he worked. As he said, my qualifications for the job were just as good as they had been for any of the other jobs I had had in Canada—"the ability to bullshit while you are figuring out how to do the job"—and once again, I was clean, polite, and usually sober, qualities as valuable to the owner of a fishing camp that catered to American tourists as they were to a contractor in Churchill. Actually this owner needed a variety of guides to suit the expectations of his guests, including a dozen Indians who really knew what they were doing, and a few old white guides with broken fingernails who chewed tobacco for those guests who liked to feel they were being guided by a local character. I was one of those hired for guests, fishermen with wives, mostly, who wanted the shore lunch cooked by guides who had washed their hands first. Bob recommended me to his boss, Barney Lamm, and the spring of 1957 found me guiding in Canada's north woods for the benefit of some rich Americans who had paid a lot of money for the privilege of having me guide them. For three days the situation was ludicrous: not only did I know nothing about the geography of northwest Ontario, but the only fishing I had ever done was in the Thames at Hampton Court, where a three-ounce roach or dace is a respectable fish. Here the northern pike could reach twenty pounds, and the pickerel ten. I had no idea how you baited a line or unhooked a fish of that size; I couldn't run an outboard motor, I didn't know what trolling or any other fishing term meant, and I had not the faintest idea of how to go about cooking shore lunch, a specialty of the camp. But Barney Lamm knew what he was doing. He assigned me to big parties needing two or three guides and I watched and listened and sweated, and Barney switched me around as soon as my guests complained, and by the fourth day I knew enough to know when I could confess my ignorance. After two weeks I was burnt black, and looked and sounded like a guide; by midsummer, some of the departing guests were telling new guests that they should ask for me. Bob was right; it was a simple job, as long as you kept your wits about you. A Canadian guest would have seen through me immediately—I still had a strong south London accent—but the few Canadians got Indian guides, which they expected. Occasionally we got some real fishermen and the owner never let me near them, either. For most people, most of the time, I was what they expected to find up in Canada, a guy with a funny accent who knew the country. The highlight of that aspect of my experience was having a guest from Texas, a man who had made millions pumping mud into a hole in the ground and catching the oil that came up at another hole a half-mile away, or so he said, explain to me the governing structure of Canada. The country, he told me, is run by the King of England, who tells the governor what he wants Canada to do. I said there is a parliament here, too. He said, they don't know from shit, they're just puppets, take it from me, the King's the one in charge.

At the end of the summer I felt that I was finally baptized into the country. I had a Canadian university degree and a licence issued by the Ontario government permitting me to operate as a guide for foreigners. I belonged as much in Manitoba as I did in Mitcham.

The summer of guiding was an experience so intense that I made several attempts to write about it, and managed one short story, but it was another thirty-five years before I realized it was the material I needed to finish off *Moodie's Tale*, a novel I had started twenty years before.

Ball Lake Lodge is closed now, closed by Barney Lamm when he learned that the English River system, of which Ball Lake was a part, had been polluted by the mercury discharged by the paper companies. As someone said to me once, "There are lakes up there which the white man destroyed before he arrived." Without Ball Lake Lodge to provide employment, the Indian settlement at Grassy Narrows, a viable community before the white man arrived in the nineteenth century, has now become part of the Indian "problem," and needs government help to survive.

I'm glad I was there before all that. Working with other guides every day, even for four short months, made it impossible afterwards for me to listen to generalizations about Indians, either the demonizing of them as Stone Age people who can't hold their liquor, or the romanticizing of them as a people wholly virtuous by nature who have been corrupted by the white man. Joe Loon, Matthew Beaver, and Ed Hyacinth were individuals, too complicated in themselves, too different from me and each other, and too hard to know for me to remember them as the "Indians." They were some of the people I worked with that summer.

I left the fishing camp, and Manitoba, and the world of work, and entered the graduate school in Toronto and met Valerie, who was working in the Park Plaza bookshop. The following summer we got married and I took a job teaching at the Ryerson Institute of Technology, and in November 1959, our daughter Tory was born.

Three days later I got the news that my father had died.

Six months after that I had saved up enough money to take my new family home to meet the family I had left.

Post Script

MITCHAM COUNTY SCHOOL for Boys no longer exists. After trying to instil in us the values of the public school, including fond loyalty to the alma mater, the authorities then calmly wiped the school out in some kind of educational restructuring. The boys who went to Mitcham County School have had the "alma mater" part of their history erased. (What would have been the outcry if the authorities had wiped out Winchester, say, let alone Eton or Harrow? The fact that half the cabinet, whether Labour or Conservative, went to one of those famous public schools meant there was no chance of that.)

But the Old Mitchamians exist, and forty years later I went to a school reunion. It came about like this:

I received a letter in 1991 from Ray Hampton who was on holiday in Cheltenham, England. He had been reading a detective story, he said, and had noticed that half the characters in the book had the names of people he had been to school with, so he looked at the cover and saw that he had been to school with the author, too.

I had been expecting this letter for a few years because there were eight of these books out there by then, all of them containing the names of at least one of the boys I knew in Mitcham County School.

When I wrote my first book I had no problem naming the hero, but none of the other names sounded real until I hit on the notion of using the names of my old schoolmates, the ones I liked. Thus Sergeant Gatenby got his name not from a well-known Toronto entrepreneur of the arts, as many have assumed, but from Blob Gatenby, a cheerful, chubby kid in 5A who used to sit on my left, in front, and was in my tent at harvest camp, and who made me go to see *Fantasia*. Peastick Churcher became an English police inspector in another book, followed in the next by another suspect, Tony ("Harry") Harold, who at harvest camp had taken the trouble to explain to me, incorrectly, the difference between jazz and swing. Joe Ockenden had his day as a forger of Canadian art; Tats Atterbury, Chimp Simpson, Muggo Munnings—they are all there.

When I got the letter from Ray Hampton, I was rather eerily in the middle of my next book in which Hambone plays the part of a klutzy police cadet. I wrote back saying how pleased I was to get his letter, and he replied saying that the Old Boys held a reunion every year in a room over a pub off the Strand in the last week of December, and if ever I was in England at that time, I should come along. He said that only about thirty or forty attended, because the school had been closed down shortly after we left, so the Old Mitchamians was a shrinking society.

I put the letter away: there was no question of flying across the Atlantic to drink three pints of beer in a room over a pub. But by an amazing stroke of management it turned out that I was needed that week in London to read the proofs of a book, so on Friday, December 6, I was sitting in a hotel in Russell Square, wondering when to start out and what to expect. I was very nervous. How would I recognize anyone? More to the point, although I had needed only their names, had I by chance chosen them because, although I hadn't seen them for forty years, they seemed right for the parts?

At 5:45 p.m., I walked through the door of the upstairs room of the pub and a man shouted, "Here he is!" and I was shaking hands, more or less simultaneously, with three elderly men, all grinning like fools. Within minutes I had identified Peastick and even managed to call him Bert, which I had never done before. Hambone was there; Joe wasn't, but his younger brother, Little Joe, was, and there in a corner were Lennie Glover and Alan Dawson. (Stan had died suddenly in his forties, at his desk.)

Half an hour after that, three fifteen-year-old boys, Hambone, Peastick, and me, were drinking beer and remembering, and I had relaxed. No one had really changed, and there was no connection at all between these people and my characters. It's true that Hambone had been a brilliant soccer player, and I, who had desperately wanted to be, had been no good at all, but surely that had nothing to do with my using him as a klutzy police cadet? True, too, that Peastick could now have passed for a retired police inspector, but the real, witty Peastick, who had once made fun of my first long trousers, was nothing like the stolid humourless character in my book.

Hambone, Peastick, and I were the last to leave. I had had a wonderful time and got everything I came for, but the next day Hambone called my hotel saying it wasn't enough, so the three of us met again in a West End restaurant on Monday night and had another fine evening, getting down to remembering all the slights we had suffered as scholarship boys with the wrong accents at the county school.

At ten o'clock we were walking across Leicester Square to the tube station on our way home when we ran across a huge, oddly dressed crowd. I recognized them immediately from Toronto's Hallowe'en parades—it was a convention of transvestites, a lot of hairy carpenters dressed up as beauty queens.

It was easy to see through their disguises. But no one could have known that among the onlookers of this dress-up were three fifteen-year-old boys, themselves wearing the face masks and dressed up in the clothes of three elderly gents on a night out.

I've lived in Canada now for more than two-thirds of my life; my children are Canadian and I'm pleased to be often taken for one myself. At the University of Manitoba I acquired an enlarged vocabulary, inflecting the new words as I heard them. I now pronounce words depending on where I first heard them, in Mitcham or in Manitoba. Some words like "pastoral" slip about in the mouth, causing me to stumble. Long *a* or short? I wonder, and I choose still, each time. The result after forty-seven years here is an accent which my students used to guess was Australian, which depressed me then, though it doesn't now. Socially and politically—in all the ways that matter—I am Canadian, but I retain my British or Common Market passport because I go back often and the line-up at the Immigration counter at Heathrow is much shorter for people with local passports, and because, although I am a long way from Lambeth now, that's where I was born.